SKILLET SUPPERS

GOOD
HOUSEKEEPING

SKILLET
SUPPERS

65 DELICIOUS RECIPES

★ GOOD FOOD GUARANTEED ★

HEARST
books

HEARSTBOOKS

An Imprint of Sterling Publishing Co., Inc.
1166 Avenue of the Americas
New York, NY 10036

ISBN 978-1-61837-236-9

The Good Housekeeping Cookbook Seal guarantees that the recipes in this publication meet the strict
standards of the Good Housekeeping Institute. The Institute has been a source of reliable information
and a consumer advocate since 1900, and established its seal of approval in 1909. Every recipe in
this publication has been triple-tested for ease, reliability, and great taste by the Institute.

Distributed in Canada by Sterling Publishing Co., Inc.
c/o Canadian Manda Group, 664 Annette Street
Toronto, Ontario M6S 2C8, Canada
Distributed in Australia by NewSouth Books
45 Beach Street, Coogee, NSW 2034, Australia

For information about custom editions, special sales, and premium and corporate purchases,
please contact Sterling Special Sales at 800-805-5489 or specialsales@sterlingpublishing.com.

Manufactured in China

4 6 8 10 9 7 5 3

sterlingpublishing.com
goodhousekeeping.com

Cover Design: Chris Thompson
Interior Design: Barbara Balch
Project Editor: Carol Prager

GOOD HOUSEKEEPING
Jane Francisco
EDITOR IN CHIEF
Melissa Geurts
DESIGN DIRECTOR
Susan Westmoreland
FOOD DIRECTOR
Sharon Franke
KITCHEN APPLIANCES & TECHNOLOGY DIRECTOR
THE GOOD HOUSEKEEPING INSTITUTE

CONTENTS

Oatmeal-Chocolate Chip
Cookie Pizza (page 112)

Foreword

If there were an Academy Award for cookware, skillets would win the Most Versatile Performer in a Leading Role.

Consider *Good Housekeeping Skillet Suppers* the tribute your pan deserves. At *Good Housekeeping*, featuring easy, family-friendly food has always been part of our mission. For this book, we've collected sixty-five favorite recipes that showcase the skillet's ability to serve up delicious food for dinner (and breakfast and lunch, too!).

Want to get supper on the table after a hard day at the office? In one pan, you can toss together favorites like Chicken Caprese, Crispy Sesame Pork, or Deep-Dish Veggie Supreme Pizza; most can be prepared in 30 minutes—or less!

And, as a bonus, you'll find recipes that will end your meals on an exquisite note, from a simple Carrot Cake Skillet Blondie and Oatmeal-Chocolate Chip Cookie Pizza to a festive Made-Over Mock Baked Alaska Torte.

In the introduction, you'll find advice on choosing and caring for your skillet, as well as skillet hacks, like chopping nuts and pressing panini.

Our goal is to make your life easier. These skillet recipes make cooking simpler by streamlining menu planning, shopping, and cleanup. So open to any page of *Good Housekeeping Skillet Suppers* and cook up a delicious dish that's ready when you are.

SUSAN WESTMORELAND
Food Director, *Good Housekeeping*

Introduction

Let's give the humble skillet a round of applause.
As an indispensable kitchen tool, it's the pan that
has stood the test of time. We know the skillet is
the everyday workhorse to cook eggs, steak, and
chicken when time is short. But thanks to *Good
Housekeeping Skillet Suppers*, we'll tap into the
unrealized potential of the skillet, with fabulous
recipes for pasta, pizza, casseroles, and even
dessert, all custom-designed for this wonder pan.
Best of all, one pan means less cleanup—and for
the busy cook, that is reason enough to grab a
skillet and get cooking.

Six Skillet Must-Haves

Our skillet dishes are super easy, but it still
takes the right pan to do the job. Use this quick
checklist to make sure you're using the best
skillet for flawless results every time.

SIZE. Our pick is a 12-inch skillet. For food to
properly brown (versus steam) the skillet must be
roomy enough to hold what's cooking in a single
layer with at least one inch between the pieces.

ROLLED RIM. This helps transfer saucy dishes
to serving plates without dripping.

BALANCE. A 12-inch skillet is large, so a well-
designed handle will make it feel balanced. A

helper handle (a small loop handle opposite the main handle) makes lifting a lot easier, too.

STAY-COOL HANDLE. To get a comfortable grip, heat shouldn't travel more than a couple inches up the handle.

HEATS EVENLY. Heat should spread from the area directly over the flame to the pan's outer edges without overheating in the center.

KEEPS HEAT STEADY. A heavy-bottomed skillet does a better job maintaining steady surface temperature at high or low heats, which allows more control when cooking.

Focus: Nonstick Skillets

Nonstick skillets are manufactured with a chemical-compound coating that's applied to aluminum or stainless steel. Chances are you have one (nonstick cookware makes up about 70 percent of the cookware market). However, there are a few caveats to cooking in a nonstick skillet. Here's the lowdown:

PROS
- Foods don't stick, which is great for egg dishes and for delicate fish dishes.
- Cleanup is easy with no bits or stains to scrub.
- No extra fat, like oil or butter, is necessary to prevent sticking.

GOOD TO KNOW
- It's safe . . . over low or medium heat. On high heat, the finish can give off unhealthy fumes (but according to experts, as long as the pan's temperature is below 500°F, it's harmless).
- No searing allowed due to the no-high-heat rule. However, cooking over high heat is safe if you have a nonstick skillet with a ceramic coating, although the surface isn't as stick proof.
- Don't heat a nonstick skillet when it's empty.
- Replace pans that begin to flake. Our pick? A heavy-bottomed skillet with more than one layer of nonstick coating—it does a better job of retaining heat and browning food.

PAN HANDLING
- To ensure the nonstick coating lasts on your skillet, gentle cleaning to avoid scratching the surface is essential. Wash in hot, soapy water using a sponge or nylon scrub pad.

Focus: Stainless Steel Skillets

Stainless steel skillets are produced using a three-ply bond core that incorporates an aluminum center. That makes the pan a great conductor of heat.

PROS

- Searing is fine. Brown steaks, like our Steak Pizzaiolo (page 14), over high heat without worrying about fumes.
- Durability is superior due to its construction.
- Sleek styles from high-end brands boast a hand-polished, mirror-finish exterior.

GOOD TO KNOW

- Food can stick if the pan is not heated correctly (for info, see "Skillet Skills: The Pan Sear," page 17).

PAN HANDLING

- Cool the skillet slightly, then immerse in warm water.
- Apply a paste of nonabrasive powder cleanser mixed with water and rub in a circular motion from the center outward with a sponge or nylon scrub pad.
- Wash the pan in hot, soapy water, rinse well, and dry thoroughly.
- Avoid using a steel-wool pad, which can scratch the surface.
- Stainless-steel skillets are also dishwasher safe.

Skillet King: Cast-Iron

A cast-iron skillet is one of the least expensive kitchen tools you'll ever purchase. It's also the type of kitchenware that tends to get passed down through generations. But if you didn't inherit granny's cast-iron pan and want to try our Ultimate Fried Chicken Sandwiches (page 54), here's why it's time to buy one and start your own family tradition.

PROS

- It gets better with age, even after years of heavy use. As you cook in a cast-iron skillet, the pan gradually takes on a natural, slick patina that releases food easily.
- It's virtually indestructible and can easily be restored if mistreated.
- Heat retention is a special talent, making cast-iron ideal for browning, searing, and shallow frying.
- New cookware is pre-seasoned. This coating keeps the skillet from rusting or reacting with acidic food, and helps food release more easily.

GOOD TO KNOW

- It's slow to heat up and can have hot spots.
- It's heavy, which is a bit of a challenge when transferring the pan from stove to oven or from cooking to serving. Use a towel or potholder when taking a skillet out of the oven or moving it on the stovetop, and consider leaving the towel or potholder on the handle to remind yourself not to grab the bare metal.
- It needs maintenance. Without proper care, cast-iron cookware can rust.

PAN HANDLING

- Rinse with hot water and a scrub brush (avoid abrasive powder, harsh soap, and don't leave the pan soaking). You can also mix kosher salt with oil to make a DIY scrubber that can remove stuck-on food.
- Wipe the clean pan all over with paper towels and place over medium-low heat until all the moisture disappears.
- Add a few drops of vegetable oil and rub the inside of the skillet with paper towels until it's shiny but not sticky.

Cast Iron 101

Our tips for both cleaning and using your cast-iron skillet
will solve the most dire of kitchen emergencies.

SKILLET S.O.S.

If you got a rusty pan from grandma or a yard sale, or if
your pan looks dry and patchy, it's not the end of the
world. Follow these steps to bring your cast-iron surface
back to life.

- **Rinse** skillet in hot water (no soap); remove rust with a
  plastic brush, then dry with paper towels.
- **Coat** skillet, inside and out, with vegetable oil or shortening.
- **Place** skillet upside down on a cookie sheet. Bake at 350°F for one hour.
- **Cool** skillet completely on a wire rack. Wipe all surfaces with paper towels.

FIVE HACKS FOR YOUR CAST-IRON SKILLET

This killer skillet has other uses you've probably never thought of!

- **Make panini.** Heat skillet over medium-high heat. Add sandwich to center, then place
  a smaller skillet on top. When the underside is golden, turn the sandwich over and
  repeat.
- **Drain tofu fast.** Wrap tofu in a clean kitchen towel, place on a cutting board, and
  cover with skillet.
- **Keep soup warm without scorching.** Place skillet over low heat, then put a saucepan
  of soup (or mashed potatoes) in center of pan.
- **Prep nuts.** Put nuts (or seeds) in skillet, place a smaller pan on top, and push and twist
  to break up the nuts. Bonus: If you need to toast your nuts, they're already in the pan.
- **Bake pies in a pinch.** Works best with a 9- or 10-inch skillet to keep the recipe volume
  and baking times consistent.

Dijon Pork & Asparagus
Sauté (page 28)

1 Best-Ever Steaks, Chops & More

Skillet, "meat" delicious: There's no other kitchen tool that delivers the easiest, built-for-speed, best beef, pork, and lamb dinners than this mighty pan. Steak options include Sautéed Beef & Pepper Skillet with Fries, Steak Pizzaiolo, and Red Wine Steaks with Green Beans. Pork lovers will dig our Vietnamese Noodle Salad and Soy & Whiskey-Glazed Pork Chops. And if ground meat is your thing, our Taco Hero, Easy Kati Rolls, and Pasta with Lamb & Pecorino are anything but ordinary. Plus, we'll show you the art of pan-searing—a must-have skill in any cook's arsenal.

STEAK **Pizzaiolo**

This juicy steak dinner with sautéed onion, red pepper, and diced tomatoes is destined to be your new family favorite.

ACTIVE TIME: 5 MINUTES   **TOTAL TIME:** 20 MINUTES
MAKES: 4 MAIN-DISH SERVINGS

2   boneless beef top loin steaks, each 1-inch thick (1½ pounds total)

Salt

1   tablespoon olive oil

1   medium red pepper, very thinly sliced

1   medium onion, thinly sliced

1   can (14½ ounces) diced tomatoes

1 Pat steaks dry; sprinkle with ¼ teaspoon salt.

2 In 12-inch skillet, heat oil over high heat until hot. Add steaks; cook for 6 minutes or until browned on both sides, turning over once. Transfer to plate.

3 Reduce heat to medium. Into skillet, stir red pepper, onion, tomatoes, and ⅛ teaspoon salt. Cover and cook for 5 minutes. Return steaks to pan. Cook, uncovered, for 3 to 5 minutes for medium-rare or until desired doneness. Slice steaks across the grain.

EACH SERVING: ABOUT 440 CALORIES, 39G PROTEIN, 13G CARBOHYDRATE, 26G TOTAL FAT (7G SATURATED), 3G FIBER, 650MG SODIUM.

TIP
Serve these saucy steaks with a green salad lightly tossed in a simple vinaigrette.

Thai Beef & Veggie
CURRY

To make this curry in a hurry, we limited the recipe
to just five ingredients (salt is a freebie).

ACTIVE TIME: 10 MINUTES   **TOTAL TIME:** 25 MINUTES
MAKES: 4 MAIN-DISH SERVINGS

¼ cup Thai green curry paste

1 can (15 ounces) unsweetened coconut milk

8 ounces green beans, cut into 1-inch lengths

1 pound boneless beef top sirloin steak,
   thinly sliced into bite-size pieces

¼ teaspoon salt

1 can (8 ounces) sliced bamboo shoots,
   drained

1 Set 12-inch skillet over medium-high heat.
Add curry paste and cook for 3 minutes or until
browned and dry, stirring constantly. Whisk
in coconut milk. Add green beans and heat to
simmering.

2 Meanwhile, sprinkle beef with salt; add to
skillet. Simmer for 5 minutes, stirring often. Stir
in bamboo shoots; cook for 5 minutes, stirring
occasionally.

EACH SERVING: ABOUT 505 CALORIES, 27G PROTEIN,
12G CARBOHYDRATE, 40G TOTAL FAT (26G SATURATED),
2G FIBER, 825MG SODIUM.

TIP

Heat ready-to-serve jasmine rice according
to package directions, top with the curry,
then garnish with thinly sliced fresh basil
leaves.

Skillet Skill: The Pan Sear

Pan searing is cooking meat (poultry and fish) in a skillet over moderately high to high heat for a short period of time. Sounds simple enough, but there are huge benefits in recipes like our Steak Pizzaiolo (page 14) or Red Wine Steaks with Green Beans (page 20). Because pan-seared meat is turned only once, the meat has time to develop a flavorful crust while keeping it moist and juicy inside. To pan sear like a pro, follow these rules:

- **Pat meat dry** with paper towels before seasoning. Excess moisture interferes with searing.

- **Heat oil** in large, heavy-bottomed skillet (big enough to hold the food in a single layer with at least 1 inch between the pieces) for at least 2 minutes or until hot. The oil should ripple slightly before you add the meat. (Note: If there is no oil in the recipe, a drop of water should sizzle on contact with the pan.)

- **Add meat to the hot skillet.** Don't move the meat for at least 2 to 3 minutes or until it turns brown from the bottom up. This will release the juices to the surface of the meat, where they will caramelize, giving good color and flavor to the dish.

- **Turn meat over.** Continue cooking to desired doneness.

- **Transfer meat** to serving plates as soon as it is done to prevent overcooking. For larger steaks that will be sliced before serving, let meat stand on a cutting board for 5 minutes to allow the juices to redistribute in the meat.

Sautéed Beef & Pepper Skillet
WITH FRIES

Peruvian fare fuses Chinese, Japanese, and Latin cuisines.
That may sound exotic, but you probably have most
of the ingredients needed to whip up this sensational dish.

ACTIVE TIME: 20 MINUTES   **TOTAL TIME:** 50 MINUTES
MAKES: 4 MAIN-DISH SERVINGS

1   pound boneless beef sirloin steak, thinly sliced into bite-size pieces

3   tablespoons soy sauce

2   tablespoons apple cider vinegar

3   garlic cloves, crushed with press

1   tablespoon fresh ginger, grated and peeled

1   teaspoon ground cumin

12   ounces frozen french fries

3   tablespoons vegetable oil

1   large yellow pepper, thinly sliced

1   small red onion, thinly sliced

2   plum tomatoes, halved and thinly sliced

Chopped fresh parsley, for garnish

1 In large resealable plastic bag, combine beef, soy sauce, vinegar, garlic, ginger, and cumin. Seal bag and let stand for 20 minutes or refrigerate for up to overnight.

2 Meanwhile, cook french fries as label directs.

3 In 12-inch skillet, heat oil over medium-high heat until hot. Drain beef, discarding marinade; add to skillet (oil may splatter). Cook for 3 minutes or until browned, stirring twice. Transfer beef to plate.

4 To same skillet, add pepper and onion. Cook for 5 minutes or until almost tender, stirring occasionally. Stir in tomatoes and beef; cook for 2 minutes or until heated through. Remove from heat. Fold in fries and garnish with parsley. Serve immediately.

EACH SERVING: ABOUT 390 CALORIES, 26G PROTEIN, 28G CARBOHYDRATE, 19G TOTAL FAT (3G SATURATED), 3G FIBER, 605MG SODIUM.

TIP

Buy a 24-ounce bag of frozen fries for this recipe (you'll use half the bag).

Red Wine Steaks
WITH GREEN BEANS

Got leftover red wine? Whip up a sumptuous steak dinner
with a shallot and tarragon pan sauce in less than 30 minutes.

ACTIVE TIME: 15 MINUTES   **TOTAL TIME:** 25 MINUTES
MAKES: 4 MAIN-DISH SERVINGS

4   boneless beef strip steaks, each 1-inch thick
    (1½ pounds total)

Salt

Ground black pepper

1   tablespoon butter

1   bag (12 ounces) microwave-in-the-bag
    green beans

1   teaspoon red wine vinegar

2   shallots, finely chopped

1   cup dry red wine

¼   cup packed fresh tarragon leaves,
    finely chopped

1 Pat steaks dry. Sprinkle both sides of steaks
with ¼ teaspoon each salt and pepper.

2 In 12-inch skillet, melt ½ tablespoon butter
over medium-high heat. Add steaks; cook for
7 minutes for medium-rare or until desired
doneness, turning once.

3 Meanwhile, cook green beans in microwave as
label directs. Transfer to large bowl and toss with
vinegar, ⅛ teaspoon salt, ⅛ teaspoon pepper, and
1 tablespoon shallots.

4 Transfer steaks to plate. Reduce heat to
medium-low and add remaining shallots to skillet.
Cook for 5 minutes or until tender, stirring
occasionally.

5 Add wine, increase heat to medium-high, and
simmer for 2 minutes, stirring until browned bits
are loosened from bottom of pan. Remove from
heat; stir in tarragon, any accumulated steak
juices, and remaining butter until butter melts.

6 To serve, slice steak across the grain. Divide
steak and green beans among four main-dish
serving plates. Spoon sauce over steak and serve.

EACH SERVING: ABOUT 455 CALORIES, 37G PROTEIN,
9G CARBOHYDRATE, 29G TOTAL FAT (11G SATURATED),
2G FIBER, 340MG SODIUM.

Tangerine BEEF

Marinating flank steak in a garlicky ginger-tangerine sauce
gives this dish its Chinese-takeout taste.

ACTIVE TIME: 30 MINUTES   **TOTAL TIME:** 35 MINUTES
MAKES: 4 MAIN-DISH SERVINGS

1   cup long-grain white rice

2   tangerines

2   garlic cloves, crushed with press

1   tablespoon oyster sauce

1   teaspoon honey

½   teaspoon ground ginger

¼   teaspoon Chinese five-spice powder

Salt

¼   teaspoon ground black pepper

1   pound beef flank steak, cut in half
    lengthwise and thinly sliced across the grain

2   tablespoons vegetable oil

12 ounces cremini mushrooms, thinly sliced

12 ounces snow peas

4   green onions, cut into 1-inch pieces

1 Prepare rice as label directs. Meanwhile, with
vegetable peeler, remove peel from 1 tangerine
in strips. From both tangerines, squeeze ½ cup
juice. In large resealable plastic bag, combine
orange peel and juice, half of garlic, oyster sauce,
honey, ginger, five-spice powder, ¼ teaspoon each
salt and pepper, and beef. Seal bag and let stand
for 10 minutes.

2 Meanwhile, in 12-inch skillet, heat 1 tablespoon
oil over medium-high heat until hot. Add
mushrooms, remaining garlic, and ⅛ teaspoon
salt. Cook for 3 to 4 minutes or until mushrooms
are tender, stirring occasionally. Add snow peas
and cook for 3 minutes or until snow peas are
tender-crisp, stirring occasionally. Transfer to
large plate.

3 To same skillet, add remaining 1 tablespoon oil
and heat over medium-high heat until hot. Add
beef and marinade; cook for 4 minutes or until
beef is no longer pink, stirring occasionally. Add
mushroom mixture and green onions, tossing
to combine. Cook for 2 minutes or until green
onions have wilted, stirring occasionally. Serve
with rice.

EACH SERVING: ABOUT 505 CALORIES, 33G PROTEIN,
58G CARBOHYDRATE, 16G TOTAL FAT (4G SATURATED),
4G FIBER, 415MG SODIUM.

PASTA WITH
Lamb & Pecorino

This fragrant pasta dish with ground lamb, cumin, coriander, tomato, and mint takes its flavor cue from the Mediterranean.

ACTIVE TIME: 15 MINUTES   **TOTAL TIME:** 30 MINUTES
MAKES: 6 MAIN-DISH SERVINGS

1   pound ground lamb

Salt

1   small red pepper, finely chopped

3   garlic cloves, finely chopped

1½ teaspoons ground cumin

1½ teaspoons ground coriander

1   pound penne rigate

3   tablespoons tomato paste

1   cup fresh mint leaves, finely chopped

½   cup freshly grated Pecorino cheese

1   Heat 12-inch skillet over medium-high heat. Add lamb; sprinkle with ½ teaspoon salt. Cook for 3 minutes or until lamb is browned, breaking up meat with side of spoon. Add red pepper, garlic, cumin, coriander, and pinch salt; cook for 3 minutes or until beginning to soften, stirring occasionally.

2   Meanwhile, cook pasta as label directs. Drain pasta, reserving *1 cup cooking water*. Return pasta to pot. Stir in tomato paste and cooking water. Cook for 2 minutes, stirring.

3   Stir lamb mixture, mint, and Pecorino into pot with pasta; toss to combine.

EACH SERVING: ABOUT 560 CALORIES, 28G PROTEIN, 61G CARBOHYDRATE, 22G TOTAL FAT (10G SATURATED), 4G FIBER, 545MG SODIUM.

Taco HERO

Swap typical tortillas for toasted hero rolls and bingo—
the perfect hot beef sandwich.

ACTIVE TIME: 10 MINUTES   **TOTAL TIME:** 20 MINUTES
MAKES: 4 MAIN-DISH SERVINGS

1 tablespoon canola oil

1 small onion, finely chopped

1¼ pounds lean (90 percent) ground beef

2 teaspoons chili powder

1 teaspoon ground cumin

½ teaspoon salt

2 medium tomatoes, chopped

4 hero rolls, lightly toasted

Cheddar cheese and lettuce, shredded,
  for serving

Crushed red pepper (optional)

1 In 12-inch skillet, heat oil over medium-high heat until hot. Add onion and cook for 3 minutes or until starting to soften, stirring occasionally. Add beef, chili powder, cumin, and salt. Cook for 5 to 7 minutes or until beef is browned, breaking up meat with side of spoon. Stir in tomatoes; cook for 1 minute or until hot, stirring.

2 Divide filling among rolls. Serve with cheddar and lettuce and top with crushed red pepper, if desired.

EACH SERVING: ABOUT 435 CALORIES, 34G PROTEIN, 27G CARBOHYDRATE, 21G TOTAL FAT (7G SATURATED), 2G FIBER, 665MG SODIUM.

TIP

To cut the carbs, wrap this tasty filling in Boston lettuce leaves instead of rolls.

Creole FRIED RICE

Smoky and spicy andouille sausage transforms
typical rice and beans into a special occasional meal.

ACTIVE TIME: 10 MINUTES   **TOTAL TIME:** 20 MINUTES
MAKES: 4 MAIN-DISH SERVINGS

2   tablespoons canola oil

8   ounces andouille sausage, thinly sliced

1   large onion, chopped

1   large green pepper, chopped

3   garlic cloves, chopped

1   tablespoon creole seasoning

4   cups cooked white rice

1   can (15 ounces) kidney beans, rinsed and
     drained

2   tablespoons tomato paste

Sliced green onions and hot pepper sauce,
     for serving

1 In 12-inch skillet, heat oil over medium heat until hot. Add sausage, onion, green pepper, garlic, and creole seasoning. Cook for 10 minutes or until vegetables are tender, stirring often.
2 Stir in rice, beans, and tomato paste; cook for 2 minutes or until rice is hot, stirring occasionally. Sprinkle with green onions. Serve with hot sauce.

EACH SERVING: ABOUT 495 CALORIES, 21G PROTEIN, 68G CARBOHYDRATE, 16G TOTAL FAT (4G SATURATED), 8G FIBER, 985MG SODIUM.

TIP

If you prefer this dish less spicy, substitute smoked pork or turkey kielbasa for the andouille sausage.

Dijon Pork & Asparagus
SAUTÉ

This easy weeknight meal takes a mere 20 minutes to put together. For photo, see page 12.

ACTIVE TIME: 5 MINUTES   **TOTAL TIME:** 15 MINUTES
MAKES: 4 MAIN-DISH SERVINGS

2   tablespoons fresh tarragon leaves, chopped

½   teaspoon salt

4   thick boneless pork loin chops (about 1½ pounds total)

2   tablespoons olive oil

1   pound asparagus, sliced on an angle

1   bunch green onions, sliced

½   cup dry white wine

1   tablespoon Dijon mustard

1 In cup, combine tarragon and salt; rub onto both sides of pork.

2 In 12-inch skillet, heat oil over medium-high heat until hot. Add pork; cook for 5 minutes or until browned, turning once. Transfer to plate.

3 To same skillet, add asparagus and green onions; cook for 3 minutes, stirring. Add wine and simmer for 2 minutes; stir in mustard. Nestle pork into asparagus and cook for 2 to 4 minutes more or until meat thermometer inserted in thickest part of pork reaches 145°F.

EACH SERVING: ABOUT 455 CALORIES, 37G PROTEIN, 7G CARBOHYDRATE, 31G TOTAL FAT (9G SATURATED), 2G FIBER, 470MG SODIUM.

TIP

When slicing asparagus, keep the spears rubber-banded together. Use a chef's knife to chop off ends with one quick cut, then snip bands.

Vietnamese
NOODLE SALAD

A fabulous play on sweet-tart and spicy-salty, this simple pork-and-noodle dish characterizes the best of Southeast Asian cuisine.

ACTIVE TIME: 5 MINUTES   **TOTAL TIME:** 20 MINUTES

MAKES: 4 MAIN-DISH SERVINGS

8   ounces thin rice noodles

3   tablespoons fish sauce

2   tablespoons sugar

2   tablespoons white vinegar

1   tablespoon vegetable oil

1   pound ground pork

3   garlic cloves, crushed

1   jalapeño chile, finely chopped

1   romaine heart, sliced

¼   cup chopped peanuts and fresh herbs (such as mint, cilantro, and basil), for garnish

1 Prepare noodles as label directs.

2 Meanwhile, make dressing: In small bowl with wire whisk, mix together fish sauce, sugar, and vinegar until well blended.

3 In 12-inch skillet, heat oil over medium-high heat until hot. Add pork, garlic, jalapeño, and 2 tablespoons dressing. Cook for 5 minutes or until pork is cooked through, breaking up meat with side of spoon.

4 Cut cooked noodles with kitchen shears. Add to large bowl with pork, romaine, and remaining dressing; toss together. Garnish with peanuts and herbs.

EACH SERVING: ABOUT 465 CALORIES, 28G PROTEIN, 60G CARBOHYDRATE, 13G TOTAL FAT (2G SATURATED), 23G FIBER, 980MG SODIUM.

TIP

Thin noodles (vermicelli) made from rice cook quickly and absorb the dressing easily.

Soy & Whiskey-Glazed
PORK CHOPS

Whiskey lends a smoky flavor to this fabulous pan sauce with shiitake mushrooms and fresh ginger.

ACTIVE TIME: 20 MINUTES   **TOTAL TIME:** 30 MINUTES
MAKES: 4 MAIN-DISH SERVINGS

1   piece fresh ginger (2 inches long), peeled

2   tablespoons vegetable oil

1   pound broccoli florets

8   ounces shiitake mushrooms, stems discarded and cut into 1-inch pieces

¼   cup plus 1 tablespoon lower-sodium soy sauce

4   center-cut boneless pork chops (each ¾-inch thick)

¼   teaspoon ground black pepper

2   garlic cloves, lightly smashed

2   tablespoons whiskey

2   tablespoons sugar

Green onions, thinly sliced, for garnish

1 Cut half of ginger into quarters and finely chop remaining half.

2 In 12-inch skillet, heat 1 tablespoon oil over medium-high heat until hot. Add chopped ginger and cook for 10 seconds, stirring constantly. Add broccoli and mushrooms; cook for 1 minute, stirring; stir in *½ cup water* and 1 tablespoon soy sauce. Cover and cook for 3 minutes or until vegetables are tender and liquid has evaporated. Transfer to four main-dish serving plates; cover with foil and keep warm.

3 Sprinkle both sides of pork with pepper. Wipe out skillet and heat remaining 1 tablespoon oil over medium heat until hot. Add pork; cook for 7 to 8 minutes or until browned on the outside and barely pink in the center, turning once. Transfer pork to plate.

4 To same skillet, add garlic, whiskey, sugar, quartered ginger, remaining ¼ cup soy sauce, and *3 tablespoons water*; simmer for 4 to 6 minutes or until mixture resembles the consistency of thin syrup, stirring occasionally. Stir in any accumulated pork juices from plate. Remove and discard garlic and ginger.

5 To serve, divide pork chops among four main-dish serving plates with broccoli mixture. Spoon sauce over pork.

EACH SERVING: ABOUT 505 CALORIES, 40G PROTEIN, 17G CARBOHYDRATE, 31G TOTAL FAT (9G SATURATED), 5G FIBER, 865MG SODIUM.

Crispy Sesame
PORK

Thanks to the skillet, you only need a fraction of the oil typically required to fry pork chops to perfection.

ACTIVE TIME: 10 MINUTES **TOTAL TIME:** 15 MINUTES PLUS COOLING
MAKES: 4 MAIN-DISH SERVINGS

- 3 tablespoons lower-sodium soy sauce
- 2 tablespoons brown sugar
- 1/3 cup panko breadcrumbs
- 2 tablespoons sesame seeds
- 1 large egg
- 4 thin boneless pork chops (about 1 pound total)
- 3 tablespoons canola oil
- 1 container (5 ounces) baby arugula
- 1 cup grape tomatoes, halved
- 1 cup shredded carrots

1 In small saucepan, mix soy sauce and brown sugar until blended; heat to simmering over medium heat. Simmer for 2 minutes; cool.

2 On medium plate, combine breadcrumbs and sesame seeds. In shallow bowl with fork, beat egg. Dip pork in egg, then coat with crumb mixture, pressing firmly so mixture adheres.

3 In 12-inch skillet, heat oil over medium-high heat until hot. Add pork; fry for 6 minutes or until cooked through, turning once. Drain on paper towels; cut into cubes.

4 In large bowl, toss arugula, tomatoes, carrots, and pork with soy reduction. Serve immediately.

EACH SERVING: ABOUT 375 CALORIES, 24G PROTEIN, 19G CARBOHYDRATE, 22G TOTAL FAT (4G SATURATED), 2G FIBER, 520MG SODIUM.

TIP

For perfectly crisp pork, test the oil temperature before frying. Drop in a breadcrumb; if it sizzles, the oil is hot enough.

Five-Spice Pork
WITH PLUMS

Try this pork chop dinner while summer plums are at their peak.
It's super speedy, so you won't break a sweat.

ACTIVE TIME: 10 MINUTES **TOTAL TIME:** 20 MINUTES
MAKES: 4 MAIN-DISH SERVINGS

4   boneless pork loin chops (3 ounces each)

3/4 teaspoon Chinese five-spice powder

1/4 teaspoon salt

2   tablespoons butter

5   plums, sliced

1   garlic clove, crushed with press

1/4 cup seasoned rice vinegar

2   tablespoons soy sauce

1   tablespoon brown sugar

3   green onions, cut into 1-inch pieces

1 Sprinkle pork with five-spice powder and salt. In 12-inch skillet, melt butter over medium-high heat; add pork and cook for 5 minutes or until browned, turning once. Transfer to plate.

2 To same skillet, add plums; cook for 3 minutes or until tender, stirring occasionally. Stir in garlic, then soy sauce and brown sugar; cook until simmering, stirring often.

3 Return pork to skillet; cook for 1 minute or until cooked through. Stir in green onions.

EACH SERVING: ABOUT 315 CALORIES, 19G PROTEIN, 21G CARBOHYDRATE, 18G TOTAL FAT (8G SATURATED), 2G FIBER, 865MG SODIUM.

Easy
KATI ROLLS

These flatbread wraps filled with spiced lamb and cucumber yogurt
are typical of Indian street food—bursting with flavor.

ACTIVE TIME: 15 MINUTES   **TOTAL TIME:** 25 MINUTES

MAKES: 6 MAIN-DISH SERVINGS

½ English (seedless) cucumber, grated

1 cup nonfat Greek yogurt

1¼ teaspoons ground cumin

1¼ teaspoons salt

⅛ teaspoon ground black pepper

1 tablespoon vegetable oil

1 onion, chopped

2 jalapeño chiles, seeded and diced

1 teaspoon ground ginger

¼ teaspoon ground cloves

1¼ pounds ground lamb

2 medium tomatoes, chopped

6 pieces naan (Indian-style flatbread)

2 tablespoons butter, melted

Green lettuce leaves

1 Preheat oven to 400°F.

2 In medium bowl, combine cucumber, yogurt,
¼ teaspoon cumin, ¼ teaspoon salt, and pepper.

3 In 12-inch skillet, heat oil over medium-high
heat until hot. Add onion and jalapeños; cook
for 2 minutes, stirring often. Add remaining
1 teaspoon cumin, ginger, and cloves; cook for
1 minute, stirring. Add lamb, tomatoes, and
remaining 1 teaspoon salt. Cook for 5 to 7
minutes or until lamb is browned, breaking up
meat with side of spoon.

4 Meanwhile, place naan on cookie sheet; brush
with melted butter. Bake for 5 minutes or until
lightly toasted.

5 Place lettuce leaves on each piece of naan; top
evenly with lamb and yogurt mixtures.

EACH SERVING: ABOUT 545 CALORIES, 25G PROTEIN,
35G CARBOHYDRATE, 34G TOTAL FAT (14G SATURATED),
6G FIBER, 1,005MG SODIUM.

TIP

If you want to lighten up this recipe, sub in
lean ground beef or turkey for the lamb.

BACON & EGG
Fried Rice

Here's a great idea for leftover rice—add bacon and eggs
for a tasty twist on dinner!

ACTIVE TIME: 10 MINUTES   **TOTAL TIME:** 15 MINUTES
MAKES: 4 MAIN-DISH SERVINGS

2   tablespoons canola oil

5   slices bacon, chopped

1   bunch green onions, sliced

1   bag (5 ounces) baby spinach

3   cups cooked white rice

1   cup frozen peas

½   teaspoon salt

4   large eggs

1 In 12-inch skillet, heat 1 tablespoon oil over medium-high heat until hot. Add bacon and cook until crisp, stirring. Add green onions and spinach; cook, stirring constantly, for 2 minutes or just until spinach wilts. Add rice, peas, and salt; cook for 5 minutes or until hot, stirring often.
2 Meanwhile, in 10-inch skillet, heat remaining 1 tablespoon oil over medium heat until hot. Break eggs into pan; reduce heat to low. For sunny-side up eggs, cover and slowly cook until whites are set and yolks have thickened. For over-easy eggs, carefully turn eggs over and cook on second side.
3 Divide rice among four main-dish serving plates; top each with a fried egg.

EACH SERVING: ABOUT 485 CALORIES, 17G PROTEIN, 47G CARBOHYDRATE, 24G TOTAL FAT (7G SATURATED), 3G FIBER, 575MG SODIUM.

TIP

To make the recipe without the bacon, up the oil to 1½ tablespoons in step 1.

Chicken Chilaquiles
(page 53)

2 | Wonderful Pan Chicken

Love chicken and want it quick? Grab a skillet. Looking for something different? It turns out skillet chicken is a flavor bomb. Tempting picks include our Ultimate Fried Chicken Sandwiches, BBQ Chicken & Cheddar Burgers, and a speed-demon version of Classic Chicken Pot Pie. Or go Italian and serve our delicious Quick Chicken Saltimbocca or Chicken Caprese for dinner tonight. In this chapter, you'll even get the skinny on chicken cutlets. And if you want to switch up your poultry, our family-friendly Mozzarella-Stuffed Turkey Meatballs and Mini Meatloaves with Veggies will satisfy the pickiest eaters.

White Wine & Mushroom
CHICKEN

Serve these elegant chicken cutlets atop soft polenta
with a side of sautéed broccoli rabe.

ACTIVE TIME: 5 MINUTES   **TOTAL TIME:** 20 MINUTES
MAKES: 4 MAIN-DISH SERVINGS

4   boneless skinless chicken breast cutlets
    (5 ounces each)
¼   teaspoon salt
⅛   teaspoon pepper
1   tablespoon olive oil
1   package (10 ounces) sliced mushrooms
1   shallot, minced
½   cup dry white wine
½   cup chicken broth
2   tablespoons butter
1   tablespoon fresh parsley, chopped

1 Sprinkle chicken with salt and pepper. In
12-inch skillet, heat oil over medium-high heat
until hot. Add chicken and cook for 6 minutes or
until browned and no longer pink throughout,
turning once. Transfer chicken to four main-dish
serving plates; cover with foil and keep warm.
2 To same skillet, add mushrooms and shallot.
Cook for 3 minutes, stirring often. Add wine
and cook for 2 minutes. Stir in broth and any
accumulated chicken juices; cook until reduced
by half. Remove from heat and stir in butter
until melted; add parsley. Pour sauce evenly
over chicken.

EACH SERVING: ABOUT 270 CALORIES, 32G PROTEIN,
6G CARBOHYDRATE, 13G TOTAL FAT (5G SATURATED),
1G FIBER, 570MG SODIUM.

CHICKEN & ZUCCHINI
Mole

Fire-roasted tomatoes, chicken breasts, and a skillet means this mole is ready in a flash, but with all the authentic flavor of the slow-simmered classic.

ACTIVE TIME: 20 MINUTES   **TOTAL TIME:** 30 MINUTES
MAKES: 4 MAIN-DISH SERVINGS

1 small onion (4 to 6 ounces), cut in quarters

3 garlic cloves, peeled

1 ounce (2 to 4) dried guajillo or pasilla chiles, stems and seeds discarded

3 tablespoons roasted almonds

1 can (14½ ounces) fire-roasted diced tomatoes

½ teaspoon dried oregano

½ teaspoon ground cinnamon

13 corn tortillas

1 cup lower-sodium chicken broth

1 tablespoon vegetable oil

1 pound zucchini, cut into thin half-moons

1 pound boneless skinless chicken breast halves, cut into ½-inch chunks

1 ounce semisweet chocolate, chopped

½ teaspoon salt

3 green onions, thinly sliced

1 In blender, puree onion, garlic, chiles, almonds, tomatoes, oregano, cinnamon, 1 tortilla, and ½ cup broth for 2 minutes or until completely smooth.

2 In 12-inch skillet, heat oil over medium-high heat until hot. Add blended chile mixture and cook for 4 minutes, stirring constantly. Reduce heat to medium and cook for 8 minutes or until brick red and the consistency of tomato paste, stirring often. Stir in remaining ½ cup broth and heat to simmering.

3 Stir in zucchini and chicken; simmer for 5 minutes or until vegetables are tender and chicken is no longer pink throughout, stirring occasionally. Stir in chocolate and salt until chocolate melts.

4 Wrap remaining 12 corn tortillas in damp paper towels; microwave on high for 45 seconds or until warm and pliable.

5 Transfer mole to serving bowl; garnish with green onions. Serve with tortillas.

EACH SERVING: ABOUT 490 CALORIES, 34G PROTEIN, 57G CARBOHYDRATE, 14G TOTAL FAT (3G SATURATED), 9G FIBER, 810MG SODIUM.

Skillet Skill: The Way to Sauté

Sauter, the French verb for "jump," is literally what happens when food cooks quickly in a skillet. Sautéing browns meat (poultry or fish) on the outside until cooked through. Depending on the size of the ingredients, the food is either stirred often or occasionally. Use the following technique for perfectly sautéed Chicken Caprese (opposite), Moroccan Olive & Orange Chicken (page 48), or White Wine & Mushroom Chicken (page 42).

- Heat oil (or melt butter) in large skillet (big enough to hold the food in a single layer with at least 1 inch between the pieces) over medium (for nonstick) or medium-high heat for at least 1 minute or until hot.

- Add seasoned or coated chicken to hot skillet. Wait for 1 to 2 minutes or until chicken turns brown before stirring.

- Turn or stir chicken several times until cooked through.

- Remove chicken from the skillet with slotted spoon. Don't clean the pan yet! Sautéed chicken leaves behind flavorful browned bits (called *fond*), which is the foundation of a pan sauce. Add broth, wine, or tomatoes to the pan; bring to boiling. Reduce heat and simmer, stirring with a wooden spoon, until browned bits are loosened from bottom of pan. Voilà! You're done.

CHICKEN
Caprese

Insalata Caprese—a simple Italian salad of fresh mozzarella, tomatoes, and basil—is easily transformed into a fabulous chicken dish.

ACTIVE TIME: 10 MINUTES **TOTAL TIME:** 20 MINUTES
MAKES: 4 MAIN-DISH SERVINGS

2 tablespoons all-purpose flour

4 boneless skinless chicken breast cutlets (5 ounces each)

3 tablespoons olive oil

1½ pounds grape tomatoes, halved

3 garlic cloves, sliced

½ teaspoon salt

8 ounces fresh mozzarella balls, halved

¼ teaspoon ground black pepper

Small fresh basil leaves, for garnish

1 On sheet of waxed paper, spread flour; dredge chicken in flour.
2 In large skillet, heat oil over medium-high heat until hot. Add chicken and cook for 6 minutes or until golden and no longer pink throughout, turning once. Transfer chicken to four main-dish serving plates and keep warm.
3 To same skillet, add tomatoes, garlic, salt, and pepper. Cook for 3 minutes, stirring until browned bits are loosened from bottom of pan. Top chicken with tomatoes and mozzarella; garnish with basil.

EACH SERVING: ABOUT 475 CALORIES, 45G PROTEIN, 12G CARBOHYDRATE, 28G TOTAL FAT (10G SATURATED), 4G FIBER, 570MG SODIUM.

TIP

A side of roasted broccolini is the perfect accompaniment to this dish.

Moroccan Olive & Orange
CHICKEN

Our twist on this traditionally slow-simmered
chicken dish is ready in just 20 minutes.

ACTIVE TIME: 10 MINUTES **TOTAL TIME:** 20 MINUTES
MAKES: 4 MAIN-DISH SERVINGS

4 boneless skinless chicken breast cutlets
(4 ounces each)

¼ teaspoon salt

¼ teaspoon ground black pepper

¼ cup all-purpose flour

3 tablespoons olive oil

1 small red onion, sliced

2 navel oranges

½ cup pitted green olives, halved

2 cups cooked rice pilaf

Chopped fresh parsley, for garnish

1 On sheet of waxed paper, spread flour.
Sprinkle chicken with salt and pepper; dredge
in flour.

2 In 12-inch skillet, heat oil over medium-high
heat until hot. Add chicken and cook for 6 minutes
or until browned and no longer pink throughout,
turning once. Transfer to plate.

3 Reduce heat to medium; add onion and cook
for 2 minutes or until browned, stirring once. Into
skillet, squeeze juice from 1½ oranges. Thinly
slice remaining ½ orange; add to skillet along
with olives and *¼ cup water*. Return chicken to
skillet; cook for 3 minutes or until browned bits
are loosened from bottom of pan, stirring. Serve
chicken over rice pilaf and garnish with parsley.

EACH SERVING: ABOUT 440 CALORIES, 31G PROTEIN,
40G CARBOHYDRATE, 18G TOTAL FAT (3G SATURATED),
3G FIBER, 790MG SODIUM.

DIY Chicken Cutlets

Buy a package of boneless skinless chicken breast halves and turn them into cutlets! It's
quick and easy and will save you major bucks per pound. Here's how:

1 Place a boneless skinless chicken breast half on a cutting board. Hold it flat with the
palm of one hand; with a chef's knife carefully slice the breast in half horizontally.

2 Open the breast like a book; make a cut to separate the two halves if necessary.

3 Place one hand over the other; use the heel of the bottom hand to press down and
flatten each piece of chicken into a ½-inch-thick cutlet.

QUICK
Chicken Saltimbocca

Saltimbocca is Italian for "jumps in the mouth," and these bacon-wrapped chicken cutlets burst with sage and lemon flavor.

ACTIVE TIME: 5 MINUTES   **TOTAL TIME:** 20 MINUTES
MAKES: 4 MAIN-DISH SERVINGS

¼ cup cornstarch

8 fresh sage leaves

4 boneless skinless chicken breast cutlets (5 ounces each)

1 tablespoon olive oil

4 slices bacon

1 can (14 ounces) lower-sodium chicken broth

3 tablespoons fresh lemon juice

½ teaspoon salt

¼ teaspoon ground black pepper

1 container (10 ounces) baby spinach

2 garlic cloves, crushed with press

1 On sheet of waxed paper, spread cornstarch. Press 2 sage leaves onto each chicken cutlet; wrap each with 1 slice bacon. Dredge chicken in cornstarch.

2 In 12-inch skillet, heat oil over medium-high heat until hot. Add chicken and cook for 6 minutes or until golden and no longer pink throughout, turning once. Transfer chicken to four main-dish serving plates; keep warm.

3 To same skillet, add broth and lemon juice. Increase heat to high. Cook for 5 minutes or until sauce reduces slightly, stirring often. Stir in salt and pepper.

4 Meanwhile, in large microwave-safe bowl, combine spinach, garlic, and *2 tablespoons water*. Cover with vented plastic wrap; microwave on high for 1 minute or just until spinach wilts. Serve with chicken and pan sauce.

EACH SERVING: ABOUT 320 CALORIES, 29G PROTEIN, 12G CARBOHYDRATE, 17G TOTAL FAT (5G SATURATED), 2G FIBER, 885MG SODIUM.

Nutty Chicken
NOODLES

We pump up this Asian classic with sautéed chicken
and veggies. Swap almond butter and chopped almonds
for our peanut version, if you like.

ACTIVE TIME: 10 MINUTES   **TOTAL TIME:** 15 MINUTES
MAKES: 4 MAIN-DISH SERVINGS

8   ounces rice noodles or Chinese egg noodles

1   tablespoon vegetable oil

12 ounces boneless skinless chicken breast
    halves, thinly sliced

3   cups sliced red cabbage

1   cup shredded carrots

2   garlic cloves, finely chopped

¼   cup cider vinegar

¼   cup peanut butter

¼   cup soy sauce

¼   cup chicken broth

Chopped peanuts and fresh cilantro leaves,
    for garnish

1 Cook noodles as label directs.

2 Meanwhile, in medium bowl with wire whisk,
mix together vinegar, peanut butter, soy sauce,
and broth until well blended.

3 In large skillet, heat oil over medium-high heat
until hot. Add chicken, cabbage, carrots, and
garlic; cook for 5 minutes or until chicken is no
longer pink throughout, stirring often. Remove
from heat; stir in peanut butter mixture and
noodles. Garnish with peanuts and cilantro.

EACH SERVING: ABOUT 520 CALORIES, 28G PROTEIN,
61G CARBOHYDRATE, 19G TOTAL FAT (3G SATURATED),
3G FIBER, 1,040MG SODIUM.

TIP

For nut-free noodles, mix **¼ cup fish
sauce**, **¼ cup lime juice**, **1 crushed garlic
clove**, and **1 tablespoon brown sugar** until
well blended. This sauce is also delicious
on grilled meats, slaws, and salads.

CHICKEN
Chilaquiles

Chilaquiles is a traditional Mexican dish of fried tortillas simmered in salsa or mole and then topped with sour cream. We use tortilla chips, make a quick tomato sauce, and add shredded chicken. The result? Comfort food at its best. For photo, see page 40.

ACTIVE TIME: 10 MINUTES   **TOTAL TIME:** 20 MINUTES
MAKES: 4 MAIN-DISH SERVINGS

1   can (28 ounces) fire-roasted tomatoes

2   green onions, sliced

1   teaspoon ground cumin

¼   teaspoon salt

½   cup sour cream

1   tablespoon fresh lime juice

2   tablespoons olive oil

2   cups shredded cooked chicken

6   ounces tortilla chips (4 cups)

Sliced radishes, cilantro, and lime wedges, for serving

1 In blender or food processor with knife blade attached, puree tomatoes, green onions, cumin, and salt until smooth.

2 In small bowl, mix together sour cream and lime juice until blended.

3 In 12-inch skillet, heat oil over medium heat until hot; add tomato mixture. Partially cover and cook for 8 minutes or until slightly thickened. Stir in chicken and tortilla chips. Cook, uncovered, for 2 minutes or until hot. Serve with radishes, cilantro, lime wedges, and sour cream mixture.

EACH SERVING: ABOUT 500 CALORIES, 27G PROTEIN, 40G CARBOHYDRATE, 26G TOTAL FAT (6G SATURATED), 4G FIBER, 805MG SODIUM.

TIP

Use extra-thick tortilla chips for this recipe. They'll stay crispy when heated.

Ultimate Fried Chicken
SANDWICHES

Now you can make your own restaurant-gourmet fried chicken sammie at home, complete with five topping combos, thanks to our secret recipe.

ACTIVE TIME: 15 MINUTES   **TOTAL TIME:** 35 MINUTES
MAKES: 4 SANDWICHES

- 4   small boneless skinless chicken thighs (about 1½ pounds total)
- ¾   cup low-fat buttermilk
- 2   teaspoons garlic powder
- ¾   teaspoon salt
- ½   teaspoon ground black pepper
- 1   cup all-purpose flour
- 2   cups vegetable or canola oil
- 4   potato rolls, split and toasted
- ½   cup chipotle mayo, sliced tomato, and shredded cabbage, for serving

1 In large bowl, combine chicken, buttermilk, garlic powder, ½ teaspoon salt, and pepper. In large shallow dish, place flour. Remove 1 piece chicken from buttermilk, allowing excess to drip off; dip in flour, then buttermilk, then flour again. Place on cutting board. Repeat with remaining chicken.

2 In 12-inch skillet, heat oil over medium-high heat until temperature reaches 325°F on deep-fry thermometer. Drop coated chicken into hot oil and reduce heat to medium. Fry for 15 to 20 minutes or until golden brown and meat thermometer inserted in thickest part of chicken reaches 165°F, turning over occasionally for even browning and adjusting heat as needed. (If chicken is browning too quickly, reduce heat to medium-low for a few minutes.)

3 Transfer chicken to wire rack set over large piece of foil; sprinkle with remaining ¼ teaspoon salt. Serve chicken on rolls with chipotle mayo, tomato, and cabbage.

EACH SANDWICH: ABOUT 720 CALORIES, 38G PROTEIN, 50G CARBOHYDRATE, 40G TOTAL FAT (5G SATURATED), 2G FIBER, 795MG SODIUM.

Bonus
TOPPERS!

Ultimate Fried Chicken Sandwiches rise to another taste level with one of these fabulous combos:

- ¼ cup honey, ½ teaspoon ground red pepper, and sliced pickles
- ½ cup ranch dressing, ¼ cup crumbled blue cheese, 2 to 3 tablespoons hot sauce, and sliced red onion
- ¼ cup pesto, 4 slices provolone, and ¼ cup chopped pepperoncini
- ¼ cup relish, ¼ cup chopped sweet onion, and butter lettuce

CLASSIC
Chicken Pot Pie

Decisions, decisions! Make our classic or lightened-up version of your favorite comfort food. They're equally easy *and* delicious.

ACTIVE TIME: 15 MINUTES   **TOTAL TIME:** 35 MINUTES
MAKES: 4 MAIN-DISH SERVINGS

1   sheet frozen (thawed) puff pastry

1   tablespoon vegetable oil

1   large onion, chopped

1   pound Yukon gold potatoes, chopped into ½-inch pieces

1   cup chicken broth

½   teaspoon salt

1   tablespoon cornstarch

½   cup half-and-half or light cream

2   cups shredded rotisserie chicken

¾   cup frozen corn kernels

¾   cup frozen peas

¼   cup cooked and crumbled bacon

1   Preheat oven to 400°F. Line a large baking sheet with parchment paper.

2   Cut four 4-inch circles from pastry; arrange on prepared baking sheet. Bake for 15 minutes or until golden brown.

3   Meanwhile, in large skillet, heat oil over medium heat until hot. Add onion; cook for 5 minutes or until tender, stirring.

4   Stir in potatoes, broth, and salt; cover and cook for 10 minutes. In small bowl, stir cornstarch into half-and-half until smooth. Add to skillet along with chicken, corn, and peas; simmer for 3 minutes or until sauce thickens. Serve topped with bacon and pastry.

EACH SERVING: ABOUT 510 CALORIES, 24G PROTEIN, 49G CARBOHYDRATE, 28G TOTAL FAT (8G SATURATED), 4G FIBER, 715MG SODIUM.

LIGHT
Chicken Pot Pie

Prepare Classic Chicken Pot Pie through step 2. In step 3, add **3 medium carrots**, chopped, to onion and increase cooking time to 10 minutes. In step 4, omit potatoes, corn, half-and-half, and bacon. Add **12 ounces boneless skinless chicken breasts**, chopped; **1 cup frozen peas**; **1½ cups lower-sodium chicken broth**; **¼ teaspoon dried thyme**; and **¼ teaspoon salt** to skillet. Heat to simmering. In small bowl, stir **3 tablespoons cornstarch** into **¼ cup lower-sodium chicken broth** until smooth; add to skillet and simmer for 5 minutes. Serve topped with puff pastry. Serves four.

EACH SERVING: ABOUT 380 CALORIES, 27G PROTEIN, 31G CARBOHYDRATE, 16G TOTAL FAT (4G SATURATED), 4G FIBER, 400MG SODIUM.

BBQ Chicken & Cheddar
BURGERS

Barbecue sauce gives these burgers a great smoky taste
without the hassle of lighting up the grill.

ACTIVE TIME: 10 MINUTES   **TOTAL TIME:** 25 MINUTES
MAKES: 4 BURGERS

1¼ pounds ground chicken

⅓ cup barbecue sauce

3 green onions, chopped

¼ teaspoon salt

¼ teaspoon ground black pepper

2 teaspoons canola oil

4 slices sharp cheddar cheese (1 ounce each)

4 whole wheat hamburger buns, split

Thinly sliced green apple and microgreens,
for serving

1 In medium bowl, combine chicken, barbecue sauce, green onions, salt, and pepper until blended; do not overmix. Shape chicken mixture into 4 equal patties, each about 1-inch thick, handling mixture as little as possible.

2 In 12-inch nonstick skillet, heat oil over medium heat until hot. Add patties; cook for 14 minutes or just until chicken loses its pink color throughout, turning once. Top each burger with 1 slice cheddar; remove from heat and cover skillet to melt cheese. Serve burgers on buns with sliced apples and microgreens.

EACH BURGER: ABOUT 475 CALORIES, 36G PROTEIN, 35G CARBOHYDRATE, 23G TOTAL FAT (8G SATURATED), 5G FIBER, 795MG SODIUM.

TIP

To make DIY ground chicken, chop up 1¼ pounds breast and thigh meat; freeze the chunks just until firm. Pulse in the food processor until finely chopped but not pasty.

Mini Meatloaves
WITH VEGGIES

Miniaturizing turkey meatloaf and simmering the loaves in a covered skillet guarantees they'll turn out exceptionally juicy.

ACTIVE TIME: 10 MINUTES   **TOTAL TIME:** 35 MINUTES
MAKES: 4 MAIN-DISH SERVINGS

1   pound fingerling potatoes, halved

1   pint cherry tomatoes

4   sprigs fresh rosemary

4   tablespoons olive oil

1   teaspoon salt

1   pound ground turkey

1   cup breadcrumbs

¼   cup milk

½   medium onion, grated

1   tablespoon Worcestershire sauce

1   large egg, lightly beaten

½   cup ketchup

1   tablespoon balsamic vinegar

1 Preheat oven to 450°F.

2 On large baking sheet, toss together potatoes, tomatoes, rosemary, 2 tablespoons oil, and ½ teaspoon salt. Roast for 25 minutes or until potatoes are tender.

3 Meanwhile, in large bowl, combine turkey, breadcrumbs, milk, onion, Worcestershire sauce, egg, and remaining ½ teaspoon salt until blended; do not overmix. Shape turkey mixture into 4 equal loaves, handling mixture as little as possible.

4 In a 12-inch ovenproof skillet, heat remaining 2 tablespoons oil over medium-high heat until hot. Add turkey loaves and cook for 4 minutes or until browned, turning once. In small bowl, combine ½ cup ketchup and vinegar; brush each loaf with 1 tablespoon mixture.

5 To same skillet, add *½ cup water*. Reduce heat to medium-low. Cover and cook meatloaves for 10 minutes or until meat thermometer inserted into each loaf reaches 165°F. Serve meatloaves and vegetables with remaining ketchup mixture.

EACH SERVING: ABOUT 537 CALORIES, 31G PROTEIN, 55G CARBOHYDRATE, 22G TOTAL FAT (5G SATURATED), 5G FIBER, 1139MG SODIUM.

Mozzarella-Stuffed
TURKEY MEATBALLS

These juicy, mozzarella-loaded meatballs come together super quickly. Toss the saucy meatballs with hot spaghetti or spoon them over sliced bread.

ACTIVE TIME: 20 MINUTES   **TOTAL TIME:** 45 MINUTES
MAKES: 6 MAIN-DISH SERVINGS

1¼ **pounds ground turkey**

⅓ **cup Italian dried breadcrumbs**

3 **tablespoons milk**

1 **large egg**

3 **garlic cloves, finely chopped**

1 **tablespoon loosely packed fresh rosemary leaves, finely chopped**

¼ **teaspoon salt**

½ **teaspoon ground black pepper**

4 **ounces part-skim mozzarella cheese, cut into ½-inch cubes**

2 **tablespoons olive oil**

2 **cups marinara sauce**

Fresh parsley leaves and grated Parmesan cheese, for garnish

1 In large bowl, combine turkey, breadcrumbs, milk, egg, garlic, rosemary, salt, and pepper; do not overmix. With 2-tablespoon scoop, scoop turkey mixture and press 1 cube mozzarella into center, sealing meat tightly around cheese. Repeat with remaining turkey mixture and mozzarella.

2 In 12-inch skillet, heat oil over medium-high heat until hot. Add meatballs; cook for 10 minutes or until browned on most sides, stirring occasionally. Stir in marinara sauce. Reduce heat to medium-low and simmer for 12 minutes or until meatballs lose their pink color throughout. Garnish with parsley and Parmesan.

EACH SERVING: ABOUT 345 CALORIES, 27G PROTEIN, 17G CARBOHYDRATE, 19G TOTAL FAT (5G SATURATED), 2G FIBER, 960MG SODIUM.

TIP

To make the meatballs ahead, proceed with the recipe through step 2. Transfer meatballs and sauce to container; cover and refrigerate for up to 2 days. Reheat gently in skillet over medium-low heat for about 30 minutes or until hot, or transfer to glass or ceramic baking dish, cover with foil, and reheat in 425°F oven for 40 minutes or until hot.

Crunchy Salmon with Lemony Squash Salad (page 71)

3 | Fish in a Flash

Here's a deep-sea secret: When you buy seafood that's fresh and use a skillet so it won't overcook, you'll reel in a delicious meal every time. No need to flip the fish to prepare our Mediterranean Cod or Spanish Noodles with Shrimp & Peas. Think pink and make our Crunchy Salmon with Lemony Squash Salad, Salmon with Peppers, or Caribbean Salmon for a casual gathering. Plus, our Skillet Shrimp Tacos and Lemony Crab Linguine are the perfect picks for busy weeknights.

Mediterranean COD

Serve this dish with warm whole-wheat rolls
to sop up the delicious vegetable sauce.

ACTIVE TIME: 10 MINUTES   **TOTAL TIME:** 20 MINUTES
MAKES: 4 MAIN-DISH SERVINGS

1   cup marinara sauce

2   medium zucchini, chopped

4   pieces cod fillet (6 ounces each)

Salt

¼   teaspoon ground black pepper

1   tablespoon olive oil

2   garlic cloves, chopped

¼   teaspoon crushed red pepper

1   pound fresh spinach

1 In 10-inch skillet, combine marinara sauce and zucchini; heat to simmering over medium heat. Sprinkle cod with ¼ teaspoon salt and pepper; add to simmering sauce. Cover and cook for 7 minutes or until cod is just opaque throughout.

2 Meanwhile, in 5-quart saucepot, heat oil over medium heat until hot. Add garlic and crushed red pepper; cook for 1 minute or until fragrant, stirring. Add spinach and remaining ⅛ teaspoon salt; cover and cook for 5 minutes or just until spinach wilts, stirring occasionally. Divide spinach and sauce among four main-dish serving plates; top with cod.

EACH SERVING: ABOUT 320 CALORIES, 35G PROTEIN, 31G CARBOHYDRATE, 8G TOTAL FAT (1G SATURATED), 8G FIBER, 1,295MG SODIUM.

Fish Challenge: Is it done?

Cooking fish in a skillet requires quick thinking. No problem!
Just follow this guide for perfect results.

- **Thin fish fillets** (red snapper, tilapia, sea bass, catfish): When the outside is opaque, the fish is done.
- **Thick fish fillets** (salmon, cod, or halibut): Gently insert a small, thin knife into the thickest part of the fillet to see if it's just opaque throughout.
- **Shrimp:** Color turns from translucent grey to just opaque and pearly pink.
- **Sea scallops:** Cut into one scallop with the tip of a knife; it should be just opaque.

Lemony Crab
LINGUINE

Pepperoncini (or cherry) peppers are typically served with antipasto, but they're also fabulous when tossed with crab and pasta.

ACTIVE TIME: 10 MINUTES   **TOTAL TIME:** 20 MINUTES
MAKES: 4 MAIN-DISH SERVINGS

1   pound linguine

¼   cup olive oil

3   garlic cloves, thinly sliced

1   tablespoon fresh thyme leaves

8   ounces lump crabmeat, picked over

Freshly grated peel and juice of 1 lemon

½   teaspoon salt

½   teaspoon ground black pepper

⅓   cup sliced pickled peppers

Lemon wedges, for serving

1 Cook linguine as label directs; drain, reserving *¼ cup cooking water.*

2 Meanwhile, in skillet, combine oil, garlic, and thyme; cook over medium heat for 3 minutes, stirring. Stir in lemon peel and juice, salt, and pepper.

3 Toss crab mixture with linguine, cooking water, and pickled peppers. Serve with lemon wedges.

EACH SERVING: ABOUT 485 CALORIES, 22G PROTEIN, 66G CARBOHYDRATE, 15G TOTAL FAT (2G SATURATED), 3G FIBER, 600MG SODIUM.

TIP

Crab too pricey? Sauté a pound of peeled and deveined shrimp with the thyme and garlic instead.

Spicy Tuna Roll
SALAD

If you're bored with the same-old tuna salad,
turn it into sushi ingredients—deconstructed and
topped with thinly sliced seared tuna steak.

ACTIVE TIME: 20 MINUTES   **TOTAL TIME:** 25 MINUTES
MAKES: 4 MAIN-DISH SERVINGS

1   piece fresh tuna steak (12 ounces),
    about 1½ inches thick

¼   teaspoon salt

¼   teaspoon ground black pepper

2   tablespoons vegetable oil

¼   cup light mayonnaise

1   tablespoon hot Asian chili sauce (Sriracha)

1   tablespoon fresh lime juice

1   tablespoon soy sauce

1   tablespoon Asian sesame oil

Pinch sugar

6   cups baby arugula

2   cups cooked brown rice, cooled

1   English (seedless) cucumber, thinly sliced
    into half-moons

1   avocado, chopped

1 Sprinkle tuna with salt and pepper. In 10-inch skillet, heat vegetable oil over medium-high heat until very hot. Add tuna; cook for 6 minutes or until browned, turning once. Transfer to cutting board and thinly slice.

2 In large bowl with wire whisk, mix together mayonnaise, chili sauce, lime juice, soy sauce, sesame oil, and sugar until well blended. Add arugula, rice, cucumber, and avocado; toss to combine. Divide salad among four main-dish serving plates. Top with tuna.

EACH SERVING: ABOUT 410 CALORIES, 31G PROTEIN, 31G CARBOHYDRATE, 19G TOTAL FAT (3G SATURATED), 6G FIBER, 625MG SODIUM.

CRUNCHY SALMON
with Lemony Squash Salad

We press slices of sourdough bread onto salmon fillets
so that when the fish is sautéed, it forms a gorgeous golden crust.
Served on a bed of summer squash with lemon and dill, this
makes for an impressive company dish. For photo, see page 64.

ACTIVE TIME: 15 MINUTES   **TOTAL TIME:** 25 MINUTES
MAKES: 4 MAIN-DISH SERVINGS

1   round loaf country or sourdough bread (7- to 8-inch diameter)

4   center-cut pieces salmon fillet (6 ounces each), skin removed

½   teaspoon salt

½   teaspoon ground black pepper

1   large zucchini, trimmed

1   large yellow squash, cut into very thin half-moons

½   teaspoon honey

1   tablespoon plus 1 teaspoon olive oil

1   lemon

1   tablespoon chopped fresh dill

Fresh dill sprigs, for garnish

1 With serrated knife, cut top off bread. Cut two horizontal ½-inch-thick slices from loaf, then cut off crusts. With rolling pin, roll slices to ¼-inch thickness. Cut each slice in half and trim to match dimensions of skinned sides of salmon fillets. Reserve leftover bread for another use. Sprinkle salmon with ¼ teaspoon each salt and pepper. Press 1 bread slice onto skinned side of each fillet.

2 With vegetable peeler, peel zucchini into wide ribbons. In 12-inch nonstick skillet, heat *2 tablespoons water* to boiling over high heat. Add yellow squash and zucchini; cook for 2 minutes or until just tender, stirring gently. Transfer to large bowl and toss with honey.

3 Wipe skillet dry; heat 1 tablespoon oil over medium heat until hot. Add salmon to skillet in single layer, bread-sides down; cook for 7 minutes or until bread is golden brown. With spatula, carefully turn salmon over and cook for 4 minutes or until just opaque throughout.

4 Meanwhile, from lemon, grate ½ teaspoon peel and squeeze 1 tablespoon juice. Gently stir into squash mixture. Stir in dill, remaining 1 teaspoon oil, and remaining ¼ teaspoon each salt and pepper.

5 To serve, divide salmon and squash mixture among four main-dish serving plates. Garnish with dill sprigs.

EACH SERVING: ABOUT 335 CALORIES, 38G PROTEIN, 18G CARBOHYDRATE, 12G TOTAL FAT (2G SATURATED), 2G FIBER, 515MG SODIUM.

Salmon
WITH PEPPERS

This delicious sauté delivers heart-healthy omega-3s (salmon), antioxidants (peppers), and fiber (veggies and brown rice).

ACTIVE TIME: 10 MINUTES **TOTAL TIME:** 30 MINUTES
MAKES: 4 MAIN-DISH SERVINGS

1 cup quick-cooking brown rice

4 pieces center-cut salmon fillet (5 ounces each), skin removed

Salt

1/8 teaspoon ground black pepper

1½ teaspoons canola oil

2 limes

3 small peppers (red, orange, and yellow), thinly sliced

1 medium onion (6 to 8 ounces), finely chopped

½ cup packed fresh basil leaves

6 ounces baby spinach

1 Prepare rice as label directs.

2 Sprinkle salmon with ¼ teaspoon salt and black pepper. In 12-inch nonstick skillet, heat ½ teaspoon oil over medium heat until hot. Add salmon and cook for 8 to 10 minutes or until just opaque throughout, turning once. Transfer to four main-dish serving plates. Grate peel of 1 lime over fish.

3 Drain fat from skillet; heat 1 teaspoon oil over medium heat until hot. Add peppers, onion, *3 tablespoons water*, and 1/8 teaspoon salt. Cover and cook for 5 minutes. Uncover; cook for 3 to 5 minutes or until tender, stirring occasionally. Stir in basil and cook until wilted. From grated lime, squeeze 1 tablespoon juice into mixture.

4 Meanwhile, in large microwave-safe bowl, combine spinach and pinch salt. Cover with vented plastic wrap; microwave on high for 3 minutes or just until spinach wilts. Cut remaining lime into wedges. Serve salmon with rice, pepper mixture, and lime wedges.

EACH SERVING: ABOUT 380 CALORIES, 33G PROTEIN, 33G CARBOHYDRATE, 12G TOTAL FAT (2G SATURATED), 6G FIBER, 395MG SODIUM.

TIP

No salmon at the market? Try tilapia, but check it at the five-minute mark since it's a thinner filet.

Caribbean
SALMON

For a taste of the tropics, we simmer salmon in coconut milk and then serve atop rice tossed with mango, arugula, and dill.

ACTIVE TIME: 10 MINUTES   **TOTAL TIME:** 20 MINUTES
MAKES: 4 MAIN-DISH SERVINGS

1   can (14 ounces) coconut milk, shaken

2   garlic cloves, crushed with press

¼   teaspoon black pepper

1   pound salmon fillet, skin removed and cut into 1-inch cubes

½   teaspoon salt

3   cups cooked rice

1   medium mango, peeled and finely chopped

3   cups baby arugula

¼   cup loosely packed fresh dill, chopped

1 In 10-inch skillet, combine coconut milk, garlic, and pepper; bring to a simmer over medium heat.

2 Sprinkle salmon with salt; add to skillet. Cook for 5 minutes or until just opaque throughout, stirring.

3 Meanwhile, in large bowl, toss together rice, mango, arugula, and dill. Serve with salmon.

EACH SERVING: ABOUT 475 CALORIES, 30G PROTEIN, 49G CARBOHYDRATE, 18G TOTAL FAT (11G SATURATED), 2G FIBER, 355MG SODIUM.

TIP

Choose a fragrant variety of rice for this dish, like jasmine or basmati.

Shrimp & Zucchini
SCAMPI

What could be better than classic shrimp scampi with garlic and lemon? Adding sautéed zucchini and tossing it with pasta.

ACTIVE TIME: 10 MINUTES **TOTAL TIME:** 30 MINUTES
MAKES: 6 MAIN-DISH SERVINGS

1   pound linguine

1½ pounds medium shrimp (16 to 20), peeled and deveined

2   tablespoons olive oil

2   medium zucchini, sliced

4   garlic cloves, chopped

4   tablespoons butter

¾   cup dry white wine

⅛   teaspoon salt

2   teaspoons freshly grated lemon peel

2   tablespoons fresh parsley, chopped

1 Cook linguine as label directs; drain, reserving *¼ cup cooking water.*

2 Meanwhile, in 12-inch skillet, heat oil over medium-high heat until hot. Add shrimp; cook for 3 minutes or until just opaque throughout, turning once. With slotted spoon, transfer shrimp to plate.
3 To same skillet, add zucchini, garlic, and butter; cook for 3 minutes, stirring. Add wine and salt; cook for 2 minutes, stirring until browned bits are loosened from bottom of pan. Remove pan from heat; stir in shrimp.
4 In large bowl, combine vegetables with shrimp, linguine, cooking water, lemon peel, and parsley; toss to coat.

EACH SERVING: ABOUT 485 CALORIES, 27G PROTEIN, 61G CARBOHYDRATE, 15G TOTAL FAT (6G SATURATED), 3G FIBER, 860MG SODIUM.

How to Peel & Devein Shrimp

Mastering this technique to prep seafood faves like Shrimp & Zucchini Scampi (above) or Caramelized Chile Shrimp (page 81) is easier than you think.

1 Starting at the head end of the shrimp, peel off all the shell and, if desired, the tail.

2 With a small knife, make a cut along the center of the back of the shrimp to expose the vein.

3 Use the knife to pull out the vein.

SKILLET
Shrimp Tacos

Grab a skillet: Taco night is no problemo
when the cleanup is this quick and easy.

ACTIVE TIME: 10 MINUTES   **TOTAL TIME:** 15 MINUTES
MAKES: 4 MAIN-DISH SERVINGS

2   limes

4   cups thinly sliced red cabbage

12   ounces small shrimp, peeled and deveined

¼   cup fresh cilantro, finely chopped

2   tablespoons canola oil

8   small flour tortillas

Sour cream, hot pepper sauce, and lime
    wedges, for serving

1 From limes, grate 2 teaspoons peel and squeeze 2 tablespoons juice. In medium bowl, toss cabbage with lime juice. In large bowl, toss together shrimp, cilantro, and lime peel.

2 In 12-inch skillet, heat oil over medium-high heat until very hot; add shrimp in single layer. Cook for 2 minutes (do not stir); turn shrimp over. Cook for 2 minutes more or until just opaque throughout.

3 Divide shrimp among tortillas; serve with cabbage, sour cream, hot pepper sauce, and lime wedges.

EACH SERVING: ABOUT 385 CALORIES, 19G PROTEIN, 45G CARBOHYDRATE, 14G TOTAL FAT (4G SATURATED), 4G FIBER, 970MG SODIUM.

TIP

Much of the "fresh" shrimp you'll find at the supermarket has been previously frozen, then thawed. That's okay—just be sure to cook it within a day or two. It's also best not to refreeze it.

SPANISH NOODLES
with Shrimp & Peas

Toasted fideos or fidelini take the place of rice in this paella-like dish. Look for these thin Spanish-style noodles in the pasta aisle at the supermarket.

ACTIVE TIME: 20 MINUTES   **TOTAL TIME:** 35 MINUTES
MAKES: 6 MAIN-DISH SERVINGS

2 cups lower-sodium chicken or seafood stock

1 bottle (8 ounces) clam broth

1 tablespoon tomato paste

3 tablespoons olive oil

12 ounces fideos or fidelini noodles, broken into 2-inch lengths

1 medium red pepper, thinly sliced

3 garlic cloves, chopped

1 teaspoon smoked paprika

½ teaspoon salt

1 cup frozen peas

1 pound medium shrimp (16 to 20), peeled and deveined

½ cup fresh flat-leaf parsley leaves, chopped

1 lemon, cut into 6 wedges

1 In small covered saucepan, heat stock and clam broth to simmering over medium-high heat. Whisk in tomato paste. Uncover and reduce heat to low.

2 In 12-inch oven-safe skillet, heat oil over medium heat until hot. Add noodles; cook for 3 to 5 minutes or until golden, stirring. Add pepper, garlic, ½ teaspoon paprika, and salt. Cook for 3 minutes, stirring. Add broth mixture and peas. Heat to boiling over high heat; reduce heat and simmer for 15 minutes or until noodles absorb liquid and are tender.

3 Meanwhile, preheat broiler.

4 In medium bowl, toss shrimp with remaining ½ teaspoon paprika. Arrange over cooked noodles. Place skillet on rack in broiling pan. Broil 5 to 7 inches from heat source for 2 to 3 minutes or until shrimp are just opaque throughout. Sprinkle with parsley and serve with lemon wedges.

EACH SERVING: ABOUT 355 CALORIES, 20G PROTEIN, 50G CARBOHYDRATE, 9G TOTAL FAT (1G SATURATED), 4G FIBER, 900MG SODIUM.

TIP

This recipe can also be prepared with vermicelli noodles.

Thai Shrimp & Green Bean
CURRY

Thai curry paste—a blend of lemongrass, galangal (Thai ginger), and fresh chiles—is a must-have staple if you're a serious skillet cook. We use red curry paste in this dish, but green or yellow can be substituted with equally delicious results.

ACTIVE TIME: 10 MINUTES   **TOTAL TIME:** 20 MINUTES
MAKES: 4 MAIN-DISH SERVINGS

8   ounces green beans, cut into 1-inch pieces

1   tablespoon vegetable oil

1   cup shredded carrots

2   garlic cloves, crushed with press

¼   cup red Thai curry paste

4   teaspoons Asian fish sauce

1   tablespoon brown sugar

12 ounces medium shrimp (16 to 20), peeled and deveined

3   tablespoons chopped fresh basil

4   cups frozen white rice, warmed

1 In medium microwave-safe bowl, combine green beans and *2 tablespoons water*. Cover with vented plastic wrap and microwave on high for 2 minutes or until bright green. Drain and dry well.

2 Meanwhile, in 12-inch skillet, heat oil over medium-high heat until hot. Add green beans, carrots, and garlic; cook for 2 minutes or until vegetables are tender, stirring. Stir in curry paste and cook for 1 minute or until fragrant, stirring constantly.

3 Add *½ cup water*, 3 teaspoons fish sauce, and brown sugar; cook for 1 minute, stirring. Stir in shrimp and remaining 1 teaspoon fish sauce. Cook for 3 minutes or until shrimp are opaque throughout, stirring.

4 Remove skillet from heat; stir in basil. Serve over rice.

EACH SERVING: ABOUT 345 CALORIES, 17G PROTEIN, 56G CARBOHYDRATE, 5G TOTAL FAT (0G SATURATED), 5G FIBER, 1,990MG SODIUM.

Caramelized Chile
SHRIMP

Thanks to a trio of insta-ingredients—preshelled shrimp, thin vermicelli, and bagged broccoli—this spicy shrimp dish is ideal on time-is-tight nights. Caramelized sugar lends a hint of sweetness.

ACTIVE TIME: 15 MINUTES **TOTAL TIME:** 25 MINUTES
MAKES: 4 MAIN-DISH SERVINGS

6   ounces thin rice noodles (vermicelli)

1   pound broccoli florets

1   green onion, finely chopped

¼   teaspoon salt

3   tablespoons sugar

1   tablespoon vegetable oil

3   garlic cloves, very thinly sliced

¼   teaspoon crushed red pepper

1   tablespoon lower-sodium fish sauce

1   pound medium shrimp (16 to 20), peeled and deveined

¼   cup packed fresh cilantro leaves

¼   teaspoon ground black pepper

1 In heavy 12-inch skillet, heat *1 inch water* to boiling over high heat. Add noodles and cook for 1 to 2 minutes or until just tender. With tongs, transfer noodles to colander. Rinse under cold water and drain.

2 When water in skillet returns to boiling, add broccoli. Cook for 3 minutes or until tender-crisp; drain and transfer to large bowl. Toss with green onion and salt. Wipe skillet dry.

3 In same skillet, add sugar and *1 tablespoon water* and cook over medium-high heat for 3 to 4 minutes or just until sugar dissolves and mixture turns dark amber, stirring. Stir in oil, garlic, and crushed red pepper. Cook for 10 seconds; then stir in fish sauce and shrimp. Cook for 2 to 3 minutes or until shrimp turns just opaque throughout, stirring frequently. Remove from heat; stir in cilantro and pepper.

4 Divide noodles and broccoli among four main-dish serving plates. Spoon shrimp with sauce on top of noodles.

EACH SERVING: ABOUT 340 CALORIES, 22G PROTEIN, 53G CARBOHYDRATE, 5G TOTAL FAT (1G SATURATED), 4G FIBER, 600MG SODIUM.

SEARED SCALLOPS WITH
Lentil Salad

Ooh la la! Succulent sea scallops are served
on a bed of warm French lentils tossed with kale,
shredded carrots, and a Dijon mustard dressing.

ACTIVE TIME: 10 MINUTES   **TOTAL TIME:** 30 MINUTES
MAKES: 4 MAIN-DISH SERVINGS

1¼ cups green French lentils, rinsed
and picked through

1   bunch lacinato or curly kale, ribs removed
and thinly sliced

2½ cups shredded carrots

¼   cup balsamic vinegar

1   tablespoon Dijon mustard

1   teaspoon salt

1   teaspoon ground black pepper

2   tablespoons canola oil

12 large sea scallops (about ¾ pound total)

1 In medium saucepan, bring lentils and *enough water to cover by 1½ inches* to boiling. Reduce heat and gently boil for 15 minutes or until lentils are just tender and still hold their shape.

2 Drain lentils and transfer to large bowl. Add kale, carrots, vinegar, mustard, and ½ teaspoon each salt and pepper; toss.

3 Pat any moisture from scallops with paper towels; sprinkle with remaining ½ teaspoon each salt and pepper.

4 In 12-inch skillet, heat oil over medium-high heat until very hot. Add scallops and cook for 4 minutes or until just opaque throughout, turning once. Serve scallops over lentil salad.

EACH SERVING: ABOUT 360 CALORIES, 31G PROTEIN, 51G CARBOHYDRATE, 5G TOTAL FAT (1G SATURATED), 11G FIBER, 795MG SODIUM.

TIP

You'll often see sea scallops labeled two ways: "dry" and "wet." (If they're not marked, ask.) Whenever you can, choose the dry scallops—they'll brown better.

Cauliflower Curry
(page 88)

4 Meatless Mains

Count on the trusty skillet to turn ho-hum veggies into fabulous meals. Get your greens with our luscious Ravioli with Brown Butter & Spinach or zesty Baked Pepper Jack Quinoa Skillet. Enjoy an all-star lineup of hearty mushroom dishes—Orecchiette with Morels & Peas, Creamy Vegan Linguine with Wild Mushrooms, and Mushroom Quesadillas— so satisfying you won't miss the meat. Even cook pasta in a skillet with our Veggie Skillet Lasagna and Lo Mein Primavera. With curries, pizza, stuffed potatoes, and more, going meatless just got a lot tastier.

Zucchini "Pasta"
CAPRESE

Zucchini is spiralized into linguine-like strands, quickly sautéed, and then tossed with tomatoes, mozzarella, and basil. You'll need a spiralizer for this dish—the cool tool that's as easy to use as a can opener.

ACTIVE TIME: 20 MINUTES   **TOTAL TIME:** 25 MINUTES
MAKES: 4 MAIN-DISH SERVINGS

- 3 tablespoons olive oil
- 2 pounds small zucchini, spiralized
- 12 ounces ripe tomatoes, chopped
- 8 ounces fresh mozzarella, cut into ½-inch cubes
- ½ cup loosely packed fresh basil leaves, torn
- 2 tablespoons capers, drained and chopped
- 2 garlic cloves, crushed with press
- ½ teaspoon salt
- ¼ cup roasted salted almonds, chopped

1 In 12-inch skillet, heat oil over medium heat until hot. Add zucchini; cook for 1 to 2 minutes or until just beginning to soften, stirring. Remove from heat; transfer to large bowl.

2 To bowl with zucchini, add tomatoes, mozzarella, basil, garlic, and salt. Gently toss to combine. Top with almonds and serve immediately.

EACH SERVING: ABOUT 355 CALORIES, 16G PROTEIN, 13G CARBOHYDRATE, 29G TOTAL FAT (10G SATURATED), 4G FIBER, 520MG SODIUM.

TIP

No spiralizer? You could also use a julienne peeler, or simply slice by hand: Thinly slice the zucchini lengthwise, then stack the slices and slice again to form long strands.

Cauliflower CURRY

You won't miss the meat in this hearty curry with cauliflower, potatoes, and garbanzo beans. Start with the lesser amount of cayenne pepper if you prefer your curry on the milder side. For photo, see page 84.

ACTIVE TIME: 20 MINUTES   **TOTAL TIME:** 30 MINUTES
MAKES: 4 MAIN-DISH SERVINGS

3   medium red potatoes, cut into ½-inch chunks

1   small head cauliflower, cut into ½-inch chunks

2   tablespoons vegetable oil

1   sweet onion (8 to 10 ounces), finely chopped

3   garlic cloves, crushed with press

1   tablespoon grated, peeled fresh ginger

1½   teaspoons ground cumin

2   cans (15 ounces each) no-salt-added garbanzo beans, drained

1   can (14½ ounces) no-salt-added fire-roasted diced tomatoes

½   teaspoon ground turmeric

⅛ to ¼ teaspoon cayenne (ground red) pepper

¾   teaspoon salt

Chopped fresh cilantro leaves and plain yogurt, for garnish

1   package (8.8 to 12 ounces) naan (Indian-style flatbread), toasted

1 In large microwave-safe bowl, combine potatoes and *2 tablespoons water*. Cover with vented plastic wrap and microwave on high for 5 minutes. Add cauliflower to bowl, cover with vented plastic wrap, and microwave on high for 5 minutes more or until tender. Drain.

2 Meanwhile, in 12-inch skillet, heat 1 tablespoon oil over medium-high heat until hot. Add onion; cook for 2 to 3 minutes or until golden brown and tender, stirring occasionally. Add garlic, ginger, and cumin. Cook for 30 seconds, stirring constantly.

3 Add remaining 1 tablespoon oil to skillet, then potatoes and cauliflower. Cook for 3 minutes, stirring to coat and lightly brown. Stir in garbanzo beans, tomatoes, turmeric, cayenne, and *⅓ cup water*.

4 Heat to boiling. Reduce heat to medium and simmer for 4 minutes or until tender, stirring until browned bits are loosened from bottom of pan. Stir in salt; garnish with cilantro and yogurt. Serve with naan.

EACH SERVING: ABOUT 670 CALORIES, 26G PROTEIN, 13G CARBOHYDRATE, 14G TOTAL FAT (2G SATURATED), 19G FIBER, 925MG SODIUM.

Veggie Skillet Skills

SAUTÉING TIPS

Just like meat, poultry, and fish, skillet veggies have their own set of rules. So before you try our Lo Mein Primavera (page 93) or Mushroom Quesadillas (page 95), follow this playbook:

- **Choose tender veggies** like mushrooms, bell peppers, baby artichokes, and sugar snap peas. Just like meat and chicken, sautéed veggies don't spend much time in the skillet. For denser vegetables like beets, boil them briefly in salted water before sautéing to get a head start on the cooking.

- **Cut veggies into bite-size pieces.** Vegetables that are too large will more likely burn or form a tough, overly browned crust by the time they're properly cooked.

- **Stir tender veggies frequently to promote even browning and cooking.** Denser vegetables, like cubed potatoes, should be stirred once every few minutes so that they don't fall apart as they grow tender.

EASY SIDES

Want more veggies? Pick a vegetable, grab a skillet, and try these easy side dishes.

- **Cabbage:** Slice; sauté in olive oil with a pat of butter; sprinkle with your favorite chopped fresh herbs.

- **Carrots:** Slice; cook with splash of extra-virgin olive oil and *¼ cup water* until liquid evaporates. (This works with baby carrots, too.)

- **Cherry or grape tomatoes:** Sauté with chopped fresh thyme in butter or olive oil until skins burst.

- **Tender greens** (spinach, escarole, watercress): Sauté in butter or olive oil with minced shallots; sprinkle with kosher salt.

- **Winter greens** (Swiss chard, kale, collards, mustard greens): Remove tough stems, roll up leaves, and slice into thin strips; sauté in olive oil with chopped garlic and crushed red pepper.

- **Zucchini:** Slice or cut into 1-inch chunks; sauté with sliced green onions in Asian sesame oil; sprinkle with toasted sesame seeds.

Baked Pepper Jack Quinoa
SKILLET

This creamy skillet casserole is chock-full of broccoli and spinach.
Plus, it's gluten-free.

ACTIVE TIME: 5 MINUTES   **TOTAL TIME:** 20 MINUTES
MAKES: 4 MAIN-DISH SERVINGS

1   cup quinoa, rinsed

8   ounces small broccoli florets

4   cups packed baby spinach

½   cup light sour cream

3   garlic cloves, crushed with press

½   teaspoon salt

½   teaspoon ground black pepper

4   ounces (1 cup) pepper jack cheese, shredded

1 In covered 5-quart saucepot, heat quinoa and *4 cups water* to boiling over high heat. Cook as label directs. Add 8 ounces small broccoli florets to pot 5 minutes before end of cooking time. Cook until broccoli and quinoa are tender.

2 Drain quinoa mixture well; transfer to large bowl. Add spinach, sour cream, garlic, salt, and pepper; toss to combine.

3 Preheat broiler. Spread quinoa mixture in 10-inch oven-safe skillet; sprinkle with cheese. Place skillet on rack in broiling pan. Broil 5 to 7 inches from heat source for 3 minutes or until cheese melts.

EACH SERVING: ABOUT 340 CALORIES, 16G PROTEIN, 37G CARBOHYDRATE, 15G TOTAL FAT (8G SATURATED), 6G FIBER, 550MG SODIUM.

LO MEIN
Primavera

Fresh linguine cooks right in the skillet,
making this recipe one-pan easy.

ACTIVE TIME: 20 MINUTES   **TOTAL TIME:** 30 MINUTES
MAKES: 4 MAIN-DISH SERVINGS

- 1 package (14 ounces) extra-firm tofu, drained
- 1 package (9 ounces) fresh linguine
- 2 tablespoons vegetable oil
- 2 stalks celery, thinly sliced
- 1 medium red pepper (4 to 6 ounces), thinly sliced
- 3 garlic cloves, crushed with press
- 1 large zucchini, cut into ¼-inch-thick half-moons
- 2 large carrots, shredded
- ¼ cup lower-sodium soy sauce
- ½ teaspoon Asian sesame oil

Fresh cilantro leaves, for garnish

1 Cut tofu block in half lengthwise. Cut each piece into ½-inch-thick slices. Place slices in single layer between paper towels to remove excess moisture.

2 In 12-inch nonstick skillet, heat *1 inch water* to boiling over high heat. Add linguine and cook as label directs. Drain and rinse under cold running water to prevent pasta from sticking.

3 In same skillet, heat 1 tablespoon vegetable oil over medium heat until hot. Add tofu in single layer and cook for 10 minutes or until golden brown, turning once. Transfer to plate.

4 In same skillet, heat remaining 1 tablespoon vegetable oil over medium heat until hot. Add celery, pepper, and garlic; cook for 2 minutes or until tender-crisp, stirring often. Add zucchini; cook for 1 to 2 minutes or until tender-crisp, stirring. Stir in carrots, soy sauce, tofu, and noodles. Cook for 2 minutes more or until heated through, stirring to coat.

5 Remove pan from heat, stir in sesame oil, and transfer to four main-dish serving plates. Garnish with cilantro.

EACH SERVING: ABOUT 395 CALORIES, 20G PROTEIN, 47G CARBOHYDRATE, 15G TOTAL FAT (2G SATURATED), 6G FIBER, 685MG SODIUM.

Creamy Vegan Linguine
WITH WILD MUSHROOMS

This recipe features nutritional yeast, a dairy-free vegan staple that lends a cheese-like flavor to anything from salads and roasted veggies to pasta and rice.

ACTIVE TIME: 10 MINUTES   **TOTAL TIME:** 20 MINUTES
MAKES: 6 MAIN-DISH SERVINGS

1	pound linguine or fettuccine
6	tablespoons olive oil
12	ounces mixed mushrooms, thinly sliced
3	garlic cloves, finely chopped
¼	cup nutritional yeast
½	teaspoon salt
¾	teaspoon coarsely ground black pepper
2	green onions, thinly sliced on an angle

1 Cook linguini as label directs; drain, reserving *¾ cup cooking water.*

2 Meanwhile, in 12-inch skillet, heat oil over medium-high heat until hot. Add mushrooms and garlic; cook for 5 minutes or until mushrooms are browned and tender, stirring.

3 Return linguine to pot. Add mushroom mixture, cooking water, nutritional yeast, salt, and pepper; toss until well combined. Garnish with green onions.

EACH SERVING: ABOUT 430 CALORIES, 15G PROTEIN, 62G CARBOHYDRATE, 15G TOTAL FAT (2G SATURATED), 5G FIBER, 175MG SODIUM.

TIP

Nutritional yeast is sold as either bright yellow powder or flakes. Look for it in health food stores and specialty supermarkets.

Mushroom
QUESADILLAS

Take this recipe, buy some mushrooms,
add a few pantry staples, and you've got dinner.

ACTIVE TIME: 5 MINUTES   **TOTAL TIME:** 20 MINUTES
MAKES: 4 MAIN-DISH SERVINGS

1   tablespoon vegetable oil

6   ounces cremini mushrooms, sliced

¼   teaspoon salt

½   cup salsa

½   cup frozen corn kernels

4   8-inc) flour tortillas

4   ounces (1 cup) Monterey Jack cheese, shredded

Sour cream, for garnish

1 Preheat oven to 475°F. Spray large baking sheet with nonstick cooking spray.

2 In 10-inch skillet, heat oil over medium heat until hot. Add mushrooms and salt; cook for 4 minutes or until mushrooms are tender, stirring. Stir in salsa and corn and cook for 2 minutes or until corn is heated through.

3 Arrange tortillas on prepared baking sheet. Divide mushroom mixture among tortillas; top evenly with cheese. Fold tortillas over to form half-moons; spray tops with cooking spray. Bake for 6 minutes. Turn quesadillas over and bake for 6 minutes more or until golden. Garnish with sour cream.

EACH SERVING: ABOUT 320 CALORIES, 12G PROTEIN, 33G CARBOHYDRATE, 16G TOTAL FAT (6G SATURATED), 28G FIBER, 960MG SODIUM.

DEEP-DISH
Veggie Supreme Pizza

Build a pizza in a cast-iron skillet, then throw the pan in a hot oven.
Brilliant!

ACTIVE TIME: 10 MINUTES   **TOTAL TIME:** 45 MINUTES PLUS STANDING
MAKES: 4 MAIN-DISH SERVINGS

I   pound fresh or frozen (thawed) pizza dough

½   cup marinara sauce

4   ounces (1 cup) mozzarella, shredded

2   tablespoons finely grated Parmesan cheese

4   ounces shiitake mushrooms, stemmed
      and thinly sliced

½   small zucchini, very thinly sliced

2   tablespoons olive oil

⅛   teaspoon salt

½   cup roasted red peppers, drained and
      chopped

1 Preheat oven to 475°F. Spray 12-inch cast-iron skillet with nonstick cooking spray.

2 Press pizza dough into bottom of skillet. Spread with marinara sauce; top with mozzarella and Parmesan.

3 In large bowl, toss mushrooms with zucchini, olive oil, and salt. Arrange over cheese. Sprinkle with roasted peppers.

4 Bake for 30 minutes or until cheese is browned and bottom of crust is brown and crisp. Let stand for 5 minutes before serving.

EACH SERVING: ABOUT 410 CALORIES, 13G PROTEIN, 55G CARBOHYDRATE, 18G TOTAL FAT (8G SATURATED), 4G FIBER, 705MG SODIUM.

TIP

Opt for pizzeria-style dough from the supermarket or a local pizza shop. The pop-open kind tends to burn on the bottom.

Bean & Corn-Stuffed
SWEET POTATOES

Chipotles in adobo sauce give
these spuds a fabulous smoky flavor.

ACTIVE TIME: 5 MINUTES **TOTAL TIME:** 15 MINUTES
MAKES: 4 MAIN-DISH SERVINGS

- 4   medium sweet potatoes (about 8 to 10 ounces each)
- 1   tablespoon olive oil
- 1   medium onion, sliced
- 1   can (15 ounces) black beans, rinsed and drained
- 2   cups packed baby spinach
- 1   cup frozen (thawed) corn kernels
- ½   cup green onion, sliced
- 1   tablespoon chipotle chiles in adobo, chopped
- 1   garlic clove, crushed with press
- ¼   teaspoon salt
- 4   tablespoons shredded low-fat Mexican-blend cheese

1 Prick sweet potatoes all over with fork; microwave on high for 10 minutes or until tender, turning once.

2 Meanwhile, in 12-inch skillet, heat oil over medium-high heat until hot. Add onion; cook for 6 to 7 minutes or until tender, stirring often. Stir in beans, spinach, corn, green onion, chipotle chiles, garlic, and salt. Cook for 2 minutes or just until spinach wilts, stirring.

3 Split sweet potatoes and fill with bean mixture. Sprinkle each with 1 tablespoon cheese.

EACH SERVING: ABOUT 265 CALORIES, 10G PROTEIN, 50G CARBOHYDRATE, 5G TOTAL FAT (2G SATURATED), 12G FIBER, 555MG SODIUM.

ORECCHIETTE WITH
Morels & Peas

Morel mushrooms grow wild in the spring. If you're lucky enough to find them, look for clean caps that are almost dry to the touch with an earthy, woodsy aroma. Or get dried morels and rehydrate them.

ACTIVE TIME: 25 MINUTES   **TOTAL TIME:** 35 MINUTES

MAKES: 6 MAIN-DISH SERVINGS

4   tablespoons butter

3   garlic cloves, chopped

3   ounces fresh morel mushrooms, about 1 cup (or ½ ounce dried and reconstituted), quartered lengthwise and rinsed well

1   pound orecchiette pasta

8   ounces sugar snap peas, strings removed

1   cup fresh or frozen (thawed) peas

½   cup grated Parmesan cheese

1½ cups pea shoots

½   cup microgreens

¾   teaspoon salt

Parmesan cheese, shaved, for garnish

1 Heat large covered pot of *salted water* to boiling over high heat.

2 In 8-inch skillet, heat butter over medium heat for 3 minutes or until light brown and foaming, swirling occasionally. Add garlic and morels; cook for 2 minutes, stirring occasionally. Remove from heat.

3 Cook pasta as label directs. Remove *½ cup cooking water* 4 minutes before pasta is done; set cooking water aside. Add sugar snap peas and peas to boiling water. Continue cooking until pasta is al dente and vegetables are tender. Drain well; return to pot.

4 To pot with pasta, add mushroom mixture along with grated Parmesan, pea shoots, microgreens, ¼ cup cooking water, and salt; stir until well-combined, adding more cooking water if necessary. Divide among serving bowls; garnish with shaved Parmesan.

EACH SERVING: ABOUT 410 CALORIES, 15G PROTEIN, 65G CARBOHYDRATE, 11G TOTAL FAT (6G SATURATED), 6G FIBER, 515MG SODIUM.

FRENCH ONION
Spaghetti Pie

Spaghetti pie is classically Italian—but our version
has a decisively French spin, with caramelized onions,
white wine, and Gruyère cheese.

ACTIVE TIME: 20 MINUTES   **TOTAL TIME:** 1 HOUR 10 MINUTES

MAKES: 8 MAIN-DISH SERVINGS

1	tablespoon olive oil
3	large sweet onions, thinly sliced
2	garlic cloves, finely chopped
1	tablespoon fresh thyme leaves
1½	teaspoons salt
½	teaspoon sugar
½	cup dried breadcrumbs
3	tablespoons butter, melted
1½	cups shredded Gruyère cheese
4	large eggs
2	cups whole milk
½	teaspoon ground black pepper
½	cup dry white wine
1	pound spaghetti

1 Preheat oven to 375°F. Heat large covered saucepot of *salted water* to boiling over high heat.

2 In 12-inch nonstick skillet, heat oil over medium heat until hot. Add onions, garlic, thyme, 1 teaspoon salt, and sugar. Cover and cook for 10 minutes, stirring often.

3 In medium bowl, combine crumbs, 2 tablespoons melted butter, and ½ cup Gruyère. In large bowl with wire whisk, beat eggs, milk, remaining 1 cup Gruyère, remaining ½ teaspoon salt, and pepper; set aside.

4 Uncover skillet; increase heat to medium-high and cook for 5 to 7 minutes or until onions are golden, stirring often. Add wine and remaining 1 tablespoon melted butter. Cook until wine is reduced by half.

5 Meanwhile, cook spaghetti for half the time label directs. Drain; return to pot. Stir in onion and egg mixtures. Transfer pasta to skillet. Top with crumbs. Bake for 30 minutes or until eggs set.

EACH SERVING: ABOUT 515 CALORIES, 22G PROTEIN, 64G CARBOHYDRATE, 19G TOTAL FAT (9G SATURATED), 4G FIBER, 655MG SODIUM.

Veggie Skillet
LASAGNA

No-boil noodles makes lasagna in a skillet a reality, and this chock-full-of-veggies version also features plenty of gooey cheese.

ACTIVE TIME: 20 MINUTES   **TOTAL TIME:** 35 MINUTES

MAKES: 4 MAIN-DISH SERVINGS

2 tablespoons olive oil

1 medium zucchini, sliced

1 medium red pepper, chopped

1 medium onion, chopped

3 garlic cloves, chopped

½ teaspoon salt

1 can (28 ounces) crushed tomatoes

6 ounces no-boil lasagna noodles, broken into thirds

1 cup part-skim ricotta cheese

8 ounces part-skim mozzarella cheese, shredded

¼ teaspoon ground black pepper

Fresh basil leaves, for garnish

1 In deep 12-inch skillet, heat oil over medium-high heat until hot. Add zucchini, red pepper, onion, garlic, and salt; cook for 6 minutes, stirring. Stir in tomatoes.

2 Reduce heat to low. Add noodles to sauce, making sure each piece is at least partially submerged. Cover and cook for 15 minutes or until noodles are almost al dente, gently stirring twice.

3 Dollop ricotta all over top of noodles; sprinkle mozzarella over ricotta. Cover and cook for 10 minutes more or until cheese melts and noodles are al dente. Sprinkle with pepper and garnish with basil.

EACH SERVING: ABOUT 570 CALORIES, 31G PROTEIN, 60G CARBOHYDRATE, 24G TOTAL FAT (11G SATURATED), 7G FIBER, 950MG SODIUM.

TIP

To make ahead, prepare the recipe through step 1. Keep at room temperature for up to 3 hours or transfer to a container, cover, and refrigerate for up to 2 days. To serve, gently reheat the sauce in the skillet over medium-low heat, then complete the recipe as directed in steps 2 through 3.

Corn Fritters
WITH BLACK BEAN SALAD

Go beyond the cob tonight and serve these Tex-Mex fritters.
(Don't be tempted to sub in frozen kernels: They're low in flavor and
high in moisture, which leads to more splatters during cooking.)

ACTIVE TIME: 20 MINUTES   **TOTAL TIME:** 40 MINUTES
MAKES: 4 MAIN-DISH SERVINGS

2   cans (15 ounces each) black beans, rinsed
    and drained well

1   large avocado, cut into small cubes

½   cup packed fresh cilantro leaves

¼   small red onion, very thinly sliced

3   tablespoons fresh lime juice

¾   teaspoon salt

4   cups fresh corn kernels

½   cup all-purpose flour

2   large eggs, beaten

2   garlic cloves, finely chopped

1   teaspoon ground cumin

¾   cup vegetable oil

1 Preheat oven to 225°F.

2 In large bowl, combine beans, avocado, cilantro, onion, lime juice, and ¼ teaspoon salt, and toss to combine.

3 In another large bowl, stir together corn, flour, eggs, garlic, cumin, and remaining ½ teaspoon salt until well mixed.

4 In 12-inch skillet, heat oil over medium-high heat until very hot. Add batter to oil by ¼-cupfuls, forming 4 mounds; gently press tops to flatten. Cook for 4 to 5 minutes or until browned on each side, turning once. (Be careful: oil will splatter.) Transfer fritters to baking sheet and keep warm in oven.

5 Repeat with remaining batter (reduce heat to medium to maintain temperature, if necessary). Serve fritters with bean salad.

EACH SERVING: ABOUT 615 CALORIES, 23G PROTEIN, 79G CARBOHYDRATE, 29G TOTAL FAT (4G SATURATED), 19G FIBER, 880MG SODIUM.

MEATLESS MAINS

RAVIOLI WITH
Brown Butter & Spinach

While this recipe uses cheese ravioli, it's
equally delicious with butternut squash-filled pasta.

ACTIVE TIME: 10 MINUTES **TOTAL TIME:** 20 MINUTES
MAKES: 4 MAIN-DISH SERVINGS

1   pound fresh cheese ravioli

3   tablespoons butter

2   medium shallots, chopped

1   teaspoon fresh thyme, chopped

1   container (5 ounces) baby spinach

2   teaspoons sherry vinegar

¼   teaspoon salt

¼   teaspoon ground black pepper

¼   cup pistachios, shelled and chopped,
    for garnish

1 Cook ravioli as label directs; drain, reserving
½ cup cooking water.

2 Meanwhile, in 12-inch skillet, melt butter over
medium heat. Add shallots and thyme; cook for
8 minutes or until butter is browned and very
fragrant, stirring often. Add spinach; cook just
until spinach wilts, stirring constantly.

3 Remove pan from heat; stir in vinegar, salt,
and pepper. Add ravioli and cooking water; toss
to coat. Garnish with pistachios.

EACH SERVING: ABOUT 360 CALORIES, 13G PROTEIN,
37G CARBOHYDRATE, 18G TOTAL FAT (11G SATURATED),
3G FIBER, 480MG SODIUM.

TIP

To prevent ravioli from bursting while
cooking, keep the water at a gentle (not
rolling) boil.

Margherita
PASTA

Inspired by classic pizza Margherita with tomatoes,
fresh basil, and cheese, this skillet pasta is equally fabulous.

ACTIVE TIME: 10 MINUTES   **TOTAL TIME:** 30 MINUTES
MAKES: 4 MAIN-DISH SERVINGS

1   pound fettuccine or linguine

¼   cup olive oil

1   large onion, thinly sliced

½   teaspoon salt

1   can (28 ounces) diced tomatoes, drained

1   cup whole milk ricotta cheese

2   teaspoons crushed red pepper

1   teaspoon smoked paprika

¼   cup grated Parmesan cheese

Fresh basil leaves, for garnish

1 Cook fettuccine as label directs.

2 Meanwhile, in medium bowl, mix together ricotta, crushed red pepper, and paprika until blended.

3 In 12-inch skillet, heat oil over medium-high heat until hot. Add onion and salt and cook for 10 minutes or until onion is golden, stirring. Stir in tomatoes; cook for 2 minutes.

4 Drain fettuccine; return to pot. Add tomato mixture and toss to coat. Divide among four main-dish serving plates and top with ricotta mixture and Parmesan. Garnish with basil leaves.

EACH SERVING: ABOUT 719 CALORIES, 24G PROTEIN, 97G CARBOHYDRATE, 25G TOTAL FAT (9G SATURATED), 6G FIBER, 691MG SODIUM.

Mediterranean Poached Eggs
WITH QUINOA

This delicious egg dish with a fragrant vegetable-and-tomato sauce and quinoa is perfect to serve for Sunday brunch.

ACTIVE TIME: 10 MINUTES   **TOTAL TIME:** 30 MINUTES
MAKES: 4 MAIN-DISH SERVINGS

3   tablespoons olive oil

1   large eggplant, chopped

1   small onion, thinly sliced

2   teaspoons curry powder

3/4 teaspoon salt

1   can (14 ounces) tomato puree

1   large zucchini, chopped

4   large eggs

3   cups cooked quinoa

1/2 cup crumbled feta cheese

Sliced green onions and ground black pepper,
     for garnish

1 In 12-inch nonstick skillet, heat oil over medium heat until hot. Add eggplant, onion, curry powder, and salt. Cover and cook for 10 minutes or until vegetables are tender, stirring occasionally. Stir in tomato puree; cook for 5 minutes.

2 Stir in zucchini, then nestle eggs in vegetables. Cover and cook for 3 to 5 minutes or until eggs have reached desired doneness.

3 Divide quinoa among four serving bowls; top with egg-and-tomato mixture. Sprinkle with feta. Garnish with green onions and pepper.

EACH SERVING: ABOUT 465 CALORIES, 19G PROTEIN, 50G CARBOHYDRATE, 22G TOTAL FAT (6G SATURATED), 9G FIBER, 830MG SODIUM.

TIP

For this dish, look for frozen cooked quinoa in specialty food stores. Thaw the quinoa according to package directions, then squeeze out the excess liquid in a clean kitchen towel.

Upside-Down Cake
(page 115)

5 Bakes & Sweets

Magic happens when you bake in a skillet. Cookies transform into warm, gooey desserts, like our super-size Oatmeal-Chocolate Chip Cookie Pizza and Carrot Cake Skillet Blondie. With just a flick of the wrist, seasonal fruit takes center stage in a trio of upside-down cakes and our sensational Caramel Apple Skillet Pie. Enjoy Iced Spiced Skillet Rolls straight from the pan—there's even a skillet version of Baked Alaska to try. Sweet!

OATMEAL-CHOCOLATE CHIP
Cookie Pizza

Supersizing chocolate chippers to pizza proportions
can be faster—and more fun—than dropping dough by the spoonful.

ACTIVE TIME: 10 MINUTES   **TOTAL TIME:** 30 MINUTES PLUS COOLING
MAKES: 12 SERVINGS

¾ **cup all-purpose flour**

¼ **teaspoon baking soda**

¼ **teaspoon salt**

6 **tablespoons butter**

⅓ **cup firmly packed brown sugar**

⅓ **cup granulated sugar**

1 **large egg**

1 **teaspoon vanilla extract**

1 **cup old-fashioned oats**

¾ **cup semisweet chocolate chips**

½ **cup walnuts, chopped**

1 Preheat oven to 375°F. Lightly grease 10-inch nonstick skillet.

2 On sheet of waxed paper, combine flour, baking soda, and salt.

3 In 3-quart saucepan, melt butter over low heat. Remove from heat; with wire whisk, stir in brown sugar and granulated sugar until blended. Whisk in egg and vanilla extract. With wooden spoon, mix in flour mixture, followed by oats, chocolate chips, and walnuts until combined.

4 Spoon batter into prepared skillet. Bake for 18 minutes or until cookie is golden brown. Let cool in pan on wire rack for 15 minutes.

5 Line cutting board with waxed paper. Transfer cookie to waxed paper. Cut into 12 wedges and serve warm.

EACH SERVING: ABOUT 240 CALORIES, 4G PROTEIN, 29G CARBOHYDRATE, 14G TOTAL FAT (6G SATURATED), 2G FIBER, 145MG SODIUM.

TIP

To remove the cookie from the skillet, run a small knife around the edges of the cookie, invert onto a wire rack, cover with wax paper and a cutting board, and then turn right-side up.

Carrot Cake
SKILLET BLONDIE

Have your cake and some free time, too.
This skillet recipe is just as easy—and delicious—as the real deal.

ACTIVE TIME: 10 MINUTES   **TOTAL TIME:** 30 MINUTES PLUS COOLING
MAKES: 8 BLONDIES

1⅓ cups all-purpose flour

½ teaspoon kosher salt

½ teaspoon ground cinnamon

¼ teaspoon ground ginger

¼ teaspoon baking powder

¼ teaspoon baking soda

½ cup butter

1 cup firmly packed dark brown sugar

1½ teaspoons vanilla extract

1 large egg

¼ cup walnuts, chopped

½ cup shredded carrots

¼ cup sweetened flaked coconut

Vanilla ice cream, for serving

1 Preheat oven to 350°F.

2 In medium bowl with wire whisk, mix together flour, salt, cinnamon, ginger, baking powder, and baking soda.

3 In 10-inch cast-iron skillet, melt butter over medium-low heat. Once butter has completely melted, add brown sugar and whisk until dissolved, about 1 minute. Slowly pour butter mixture into the flour mixture. Add the egg and vanilla; with wooden spoon, mix until combined. Fold in walnuts, carrots, and coconut.

4 Scrape batter into skillet and spread evenly. Bake for 20 to 25 minutes or until golden brown and toothpick inserted in center comes out clean.

5 Cool blondies in pan on wire rack for at least 15 minutes. Serve warm with ice cream.

EACH SERVING: ABOUT 331 CALORIES, 4G PROTEIN, 46G CARBOHYDRATE, 15G TOTAL FAT (8G SATURATED), 1G FIBER, 295MG SODIUM.

TIP

Store the blondies in an airtight container at room temperature for up to 3 days.

Upside-Down
CAKE

Traditionally made in cast-iron skillets on an open fire, upside-down cakes are flipped to showcase caramelized fruit. Inspired by our 1931 apricot version, we offer three choices: cherry, plum, and peach. For photo, see page 112.

ACTIVE TIME: 25 TO 40 MINUTES   **TOTAL TIME:** 1 HOUR TO 1 HOUR 15 MINUTES PLUS COOLING
MAKES: 10 SERVINGS

3   tablespoons plus ½ cup butter, softened

½   cup packed light brown sugar

1½   pounds peaches, peeled, halved, and cut into eighths; ¾ pound cherries, pitted and halved; or 1½ pounds plums, halved and cut into eighths

1½ cups all-purpose flour

2   teaspoons baking powder

¼   teaspoon salt

1   cup granulated sugar

3   large eggs

1   tablespoon vanilla extract

½   cup whole milk

1 Preheat oven to 350°F.

2 In 12-inch heavy skillet with oven-safe handle, melt 3 tablespoons butter over medium heat, swirling to coat side of pan. Sprinkle brown sugar evenly over butter and continue to cook for 1 minute. Remove from heat. Add fruit, cut-sides down, to fill entire bottom of skillet.

3 In large bowl with wire whisk, mix together flour, baking powder, and salt. In another large bowl with mixer on medium speed, beat remaining ½ cup butter and granulated sugar until light and fluffy, occasionally scraping side of bowl with rubber spatula. Beat in eggs, 1 at a time, and then vanilla until well blended. Reduce speed to low; alternately add flour mixture and milk, beginning and ending with flour mixture, just until combined, occasionally scraping bowl.

4 Pour batter over fruit in skillet; gently spread into even layer. Bake for 35 to 40 minutes or until toothpick inserted into center comes out clean. Cool cake in skillet on wire rack for 15 minutes. Loosen sides of cake from pan with mini-offset spatula or paring knife.

5 Place large serving platter over skillet. Carefully invert cake onto platter and remove skillet; cool slightly to serve warm, or cool for 2 hours and serve at room temperature.

EACH SERVING: ABOUT 360 CALORIES, 5G PROTEIN, 53G CARBOHYDRATE, 15G TOTAL FAT (9G SATURATED), 2G FIBER, 290MG SODIUM

Raspberry "Cheesecake"
FRENCH TOAST

This decadent take on French toast will
make any evening—or morning—feel extra special.

ACTIVE TIME: 10 MINUTES   **TOTAL TIME:** 20 MINUTES
MAKES: 2 MAIN-DISH SERVINGS

6 ounces cream cheese, softened

1   teaspoon vanilla extract

3   tablespoons raspberry jam

½   cup milk

2   large eggs

¼   teaspoon ground cinnamon

8   slices brioche, each ½-inch thick

½   cup raspberries

Confectioners' sugar

Maple syrup and additional raspberries,
    for serving

1 Preheat oven to 200°F.

2 With mixer on medium speed, beat cream cheese
and vanilla until smooth. Stir in 3 tablespoons
raspberry jam.

3 In large shallow dish with wire whisk, mix
milk, eggs, and cinnamon until blended. Spread
cream cheese mixture on one side of each
brioche slice. Divide ½ cup raspberries among
4 slices; top with remaining slices, pressing to
make 4 sandwiches.

4 Coat 12-inch nonstick skillet with nonstick
cooking spray and heat over medium heat until
hot. Dip sandwiches into egg mixture, turning to
soak both sides. Place two sandwiches in skillet;
cook for 4 to 6 minutes or until golden brown,
turning once. Transfer to plate; keep warm in
oven while cooking remaining sandwiches. Dust
with confectioners' sugar; serve with maple syrup
and raspberries.

EACH SERVING: ABOUT 340 CALORIES, 8G PROTEIN,
33G CARBOHYDRATE, 20G TOTAL FAT (11G SATURATED),
3G FIBER, 325MG SODIUM.

Iced Spiced
SKILLET ROLLS

Pop a skillet full of cinnamon rolls in the oven,
and you won't need an alarm clock to lure your family out of bed.

ACTIVE TIME: 30 MINUTES   **TOTAL TIME:** 3HOURS 30 MINUTES WITH RISING
MAKES: 12 ROLLS

ROLLS

2 tablespoons vegetable oil

1 cup whole milk, warmed

½ cup granulated sugar

2 large eggs

2 packets instant yeast (about 1 tablespoon total)

1 teaspoon vanilla extract

1 teaspoon salt

¼ cup plus 2 tablespoons butter

4¼ cups plus ¼ cup all-purpose flour

½ cup firmly packed brown sugar

2 tablespoons ground cinnamon

GLAZE

⅓ cup confectioners' sugar

3 ounces cream cheese, softened

3 tablespoons butter, softened

1 tablespoon milk

Pinch salt

1 Prepare rolls: Pour oil into large bowl; set aside. With stand mixer on medium speed (fitted with paddle attachment), beat milk, granulated sugar, eggs, yeast, vanilla, salt, and ¼ cup butter until combined. Add 4½ cups flour; beat until dough comes together (it will be very sticky). With floured hands, turn dough onto floured surface and knead for about 6 minutes, sprinkling enough of remaining ¼ cup flour over and under dough until no longer sticky.

2 Shape dough into ball; place in oiled bowl, turning dough to oil the top. Cover bowl with damp kitchen towel and plastic wrap and let rise in warm place (80° to 85°F) for 2 hours.

3 Melt remaining 2 tablespoons butter. Lightly grease 12-inch oven-safe skillet. With floured hands, punch down risen dough and turn out onto lightly floured surface. With floured rolling pin, roll dough into 20" by 12" rectangle. Brush with melted butter and sprinkle with brown sugar and cinnamon. Starting at one long side, roll up dough jelly-roll fashion. Cut dough crosswise into 12 pieces. Place slices, cut-sides down, in prepared pan. Cover dough and let rise in warm place for 1 hour.

4 Preheat oven to 350°F. Bake rolls for 30 minutes or until top is golden brown.

5 Prepare glaze: In medium bowl with wooden spoon, stir confectioners' sugar, cream cheese, butter, milk, and salt until smooth.

6 Cool rolls in skillet on wire rack for 5 minutes. Top with glaze. Serve warm.

EACH SERVING: ABOUT 405 CALORIES, 8G PROTEIN, 59G CARBOHYDRATE, 15G TOTAL FAT (8G SATURATED), 2G FIBER, 295MG SODIUM.

Caramel Apple
SKILLET PIE

Make over a classic French tarte tatin with store-bought pastry.
(Or if you're ambitious, we have a homemade pastry recipe, too.)

ACTIVE TIME: 30 MINUTES   **TOTAL TIME:** 1 HOUR 40 MINUTES PLUS COOLING
MAKES: 8 SERVINGS

1   cup granulated sugar

¼   cup apple juice

6   tablespoons butter, cut into pieces

2   teaspoons vanilla extract

¼   teaspoon salt

8   Gala apples, peeled and quartered

1   sheet frozen puff pastry, thawed
    (or Rough Puff Pastry, opposite)

1 Preheat oven to 425°F.

2 In 10- to 12-inch nonstick skillet over medium heat, cook sugar and apple juice for 2 minutes or until sugar melts, stirring. Continue to cook for 6 to 8 minutes or until deep amber, swirling pan occasionally (but not stirring). Remove from heat. Add butter, a few pieces at a time, stirring just until melted; stir in vanilla and salt.

3 Arrange apple quarters in pan, round-sides down, in three concentric circles. Simmer uncovered over medium-low heat for 40 to 45 minutes or until almost tender, pressing down apples occasionally.

4 Transfer skillet to foil-lined rimmed baking sheet. Top with pastry, tucking in any overhangs. Bake for 20 to 25 minutes (30 to 35 minutes if using Rough Puff Pastry) or until golden brown.

5 Cool in pan on wire rack for 15 minutes. Wearing oven mitts, invert rimmed serving platter over skillet; carefully flip together. Remove pan. Serve warm.

EACH SERVING: ABOUT 385 CALORIES, 3G PROTEIN, 57G CARBOHYDRATE, 17G TOTAL FAT (8G SATURATED), 3G FIBER, 300MG SODIUM.

Rough
PUFF PASTRY

In food processor with knife blade attached, pulse **1½ cups all-purpose flour** and **¼ teaspoon salt** until combined. Cut **12 tablespoons (1½ sticks) cold butter** into pieces. Add 4 tablespoons butter and pulse 10 to 15 times or until in very small pieces. Add remaining 8 tablespoons butter and pulse 2 to 3 times just to combine. Add **¼ cup very cold water** and pulse 3 to 4 times or until dough begins to come together. Transfer dough to well-floured surface and press into ball. Roll out to 18" by 12" rectangle. Fold two short ends to meet at center, then roll up from bottom into log. Use rolling pin to gently roll dough into small square, dusting with flour if needed. Wrap tightly in plastic wrap and refrigerate for at least 30 minutes. For Skillet Pie, unwrap pastry and roll out to 12-inch circle on lightly floured surface.

EACH SERVING: ABOUT 360 CALORIES, 5G PROTEIN, 53G CARBOHYDRATE, 15G TOTAL FAT (9G SATURATED), 2G FIBER, 290MG SODIUM.

MADE-OVER MOCK
Baked Alaska Torte

This spectacular layered dessert with fresh rhubarb
is the perfect choice for Easter Sunday or Mother's Day.

ACTIVE TIME: 45 MINUTES   **TOTAL TIME:** 1 HOUR 5 MINUTES PLUS COOLING AND STANDING
MAKES: 8 TO 10 SERVINGS

PANCAKE

2   cups sifted all-purpose flour

4   teaspoons baking powder

Salt

8   large eggs, separated

¼   cup granulated sugar

2   teaspoons vanilla extract

2½   cups milk

½   cup butter, melted

RHUBARB SPREAD

1   pound rhubarb, chopped

1   cup granulated sugar

FILLING

1½   cups ricotta cheese

¼   cup granulated sugar

1   large egg yolk

1   tablespoon freshly grated lemon peel

MERINGUE

4   large egg whites

¼   teaspoon cream of tartar

⅛   teaspoon salt

¼   cup apricot preserves

2   ounces bittersweet or semisweet chocolate,
     grated

1 Prepare Pancakes: In medium bowl with wire whisk, mix together flour, baking powder, and ¼ teaspoon salt. In large bowl with mixer on medium speed, beat egg yolks, sugar, and vanilla. Reduce speed to low; alternately add flour mixture, milk, and butter, beginning and ending with flour mixture, just until combined, occasionally scraping bowl with rubber spatula. Cover and refrigerate batter for 1 hour.

2 In clean large bowl with clean beaters and mixer on medium-high speed, beat egg whites and pinch salt until soft peaks form when beaters are lifted; carefully fold into batter with rubber spatula.

3 Generously spray 10-inch nonstick skillet with nonstick cooking spray; heat over medium heat until hot. Pour 1 cup batter onto hot skillet, tilting skillet to coat evenly. Cook for 3 minutes or until edges are set and underside is golden brown. With large offset spatula or pancake turner, carefully turn pancake; cook for 2 minutes or until underside is golden brown. Transfer pancake to waxed paper to cool. Repeat with remaining batter, making total of 7 pancakes.

4 Prepare Rhubarb Spread: In medium saucepan, bring rhubarb, sugar, and *½ cup water* to simmering over medium heat. Simmer for 20 minutes, stirring occasionally. Remove from heat; let stand for 20 minutes. Strain mixture through sieve into medium bowl, pressing down on solids to release their liquid. Discard liquid. Transfer spread to small bowl.

5 Prepare Filling: In large bowl with mixer on medium speed, beat ricotta, sugar, egg yolk, and lemon peel until smooth.

6 Prepare Meringue: In large clean bowl with clean beaters and mixer on medium-high speed, beat egg whites, cream of tartar, and salt until frothy. Sprinkle in sugar, 1 tablespoon at a time, beating until sugar has dissolved. Continue beating until egg whites stand in stiff, glossy peaks when beaters are lifted.

7 Preheat oven to 450°F. Lightly grease large baking sheet. Place 1 pancake on prepared baking sheet; top with half of filling. Top with 1 pancake; spread with half of rhubarb spread. Top with 1 pancake; sprinkle with half of chocolate. Repeat with 3 pancakes, remaining filling, rhubarb spread, and chocolate. Cover with remaining pancake. Cover top and sides of torte with meringue; swirl meringue into peaks with back of spoon. Bake for about 3 minutes or until golden and toasted in places.

EACH SERVING: ABOUT 560 CALORIES, 18G PROTEIN, 65G CARBOHYDRATE, 26G TOTAL FAT (14G SATURATED), 2G FIBER, 580MG SODIUM.

TIP

The pancakes can be made and frozen up to 1 month ahead (thaw at room temperature for 1 hour before using).

Index

Note: Page numbers in italics indicate photos on pages separate from recipes.

Photography Credits

FRONT AND BACK COVER: Mike Garten

Depositphotos: © AlphaBaby 70, © Coprid 9 (left), © dulsita 97

Mike Garten: 2, 11, 18, 27, 39, 49, 55, 58, 63, 67, 69, 75, 83, 96, 102, 108, 110, 116

Getty images: © Creativ Studio Heinemann 90, © Floortje 51, © Eric Anthony Johnson 11, © Dave King 46, 59 © Lacaosa 105, © Joff Lee 23, © Rick Lew 123, © David Marsden 28, © Ian O'Leary 106, © Claudia Totir 8, © Jackson Vereen 112

iStockphoto: © Bluestocking 9 (right), © Norman Chan 38, © Oliver Hoffmann 53, © Rebekah Hubbard 82, © Fedor Kondratenko 24, © Jing Lu 68, © Tarp Magnus 86, © Morningarage 42, © Oleksandr Perepelytsia 14, © Red Helga 26, © YinYang 101

© Kate Mathis: 99

© Con Poulos: 6, 21, 30, 37, 44, 64, 84, 87, 92, 104, 113, 121

© Kate Sears: 60, 78

Shutterstock: © Bienchen-s 81, © Dionisvera 77, © Hlphoto 35, © Mongolka 74, © Valentyn Volkov 115

Stocksy: © Darren Muir 17

Studio D: Chris Eckert 7, Emily Kate Roemer 15, 25, 32, 34, 40, 43, 57, 91, 118

Anna Williams: 50, 72

Metric Conversion Charts

The recipes that appear in this cookbook use the standard United States method for measuring liquid and dry or solid ingredients (teaspoons, tablespoons, and cups). The information on this chart is provided to help cooks outside the U.S. successfully use these recipes. All equivalents are approximate.

METRIC EQUIVALENTS FOR DIFFERENT TYPES OF INGREDIENTS

STANDARD CUP	FINE POWDER (e.g. flour)	GRAIN (e.g. rice)	GRANULAR (e.g. sugar)	LIQUID SOLIDS (e.g. butter)	LIQUID (e.g. milk)
¾	105 g	113 g	143 g	150 g	180 ml
⅔	93 g	100 g	125 g	133 g	160 ml
½	70 g	75 g	95 g	100 g	120 ml
⅓	47 g	50 g	63 g	67 g	80 ml
¼	35 g	38 g	48 g	50 g	60 ml
⅛	18 g	19 g	24 g	25 g	30 ml

USEFUL EQUIVALENTS FOR LIQUID INGREDIENTS BY VOLUME

¼ tsp	=					1 ml
½ tsp	=					2 ml
1 tsp	=					5 ml
3 tsp	=	1 tbls	=	½ fl oz	=	15 ml
		2 tbls	=	⅛ cup	=	1 fl oz	=	30 ml
		4 tbls	=	¼ cup	=	2 fl oz	=	60 ml
		5⅓ tbls	=	⅓ cup	=	3 fl oz	=	80 ml
		8 tbls	=	½ cup	=	4 fl oz	=	120 ml
		10⅔ tbls	=	⅔ cup	=	5 fl oz	=	160 ml
		12 tbls	=	¾ cup	=	6 fl oz	=	180 ml
		16 tbls	=	1 cup	=	8 fl oz	=	240 ml
		1 pt	=	2 cups	=	16 fl oz	=	480 ml
		1 qt	=	4 cups	=	32 fl oz	=	960 ml
						33 fl oz	=	1000 ml = 1 L

USEFUL EQUIVALENTS FOR DRY INGREDIENTS BY WEIGHT

(To convert ounces to grams, multiply the number of ounces by 30.)

1 oz	=	¹⁄₁₆ lb	=	30 g
4 oz	=	¼ lb	=	120 g
8 oz	=	½ lb	=	240 g
12 oz	=	¾ lb	=	360 g
16 oz	=	1 lb	=	480 g

USEFUL EQUIVALENTS FOR COOKING/OVEN TEMPERATURES

	Fahrenheit	Celsius	Gas Mark
Freeze Water	32° F	0° C	
Room Temperature	68° F	20° C	
Boil Water	212° F	100° C	
Bake	325° F	160° C	3
	350° F	180° C	4
	375° F	190° C	5
	400° F	200° C	6
	425° F	220° C	7
	450° F	230° C	8
Broil			Grill

USEFUL EQUIVALENTS LENGTH

(To convert inches to centimeters, multiply the number of inches by 2.5.)

1 in	=		2.5 cm
6 in	=	½ ft =	15 cm
12 in	=	1 ft =	30 cm
36 in	=	3 ft = 1 yd =	90 cm
40 in	=		100 cm = 1 m

THE GOOD HOUSEKEEPING
TRIPLE-TEST PROMISE

At *Good Housekeeping*, we want to make sure that every recipe we print works in any oven, with any brand of ingredient, no matter what. That's why, in our test kitchens at the **Good Housekeeping Research Institute**, we go all out: We test each recipe at least three times—and, often, several more times after that.

When a recipe is first developed, one member of our team prepares the dish, and we judge it on these criteria: It must be **delicious**, **family-friendly**, **healthy**, and **easy to make**.

1 The recipe is then tested several more times to fine-tune the flavor and ease of preparation, always by the same team member, using the same equipment.

2 Next, another team member follows the recipe as written, **varying the brands of ingredients** and **kinds of equipment**. Even the types of stoves we use are changed.

3 A third team member repeats the whole process **using yet another set of equipment** and **alternative ingredients**. By the time the recipes appear on these pages, they are guaranteed to work in any kitchen, including yours. **We promise.**